Money, Prices and the Real Economy

Money, Prices and the Real Economy

Edited by

Geoffrey Wood

Professor of Economics, City University Business School, UK

IN ASSOCIATION WITH THE INSTITUTE OF ECONOMIC AFFAIRS

Edward Elgar

Cheltenham, UK • Northampton, MA, USA

Published by
Edward Elgar Publishing Limited
Glensanda House
Montpellier Parade
Cheltenham
Glos GL50 1UA
UK

Edward Elgar Publishing, Inc.
William Pratt House
9 Dewey Court
Northampton
Massachusetts 01060
USA

This book has been printed on demand to keep the title in print.

Paperback edition 2007

A catalogue record for this book
is available from the British Library

Library of Congress Cataloguing in Publication Data
Money, prices, and the real economy / edited by Geoffrey Wood.
    "[Written] In association with the Institute of Economic Affairs."
    Includes bibliographical references and index.
    1. Money. 2. Prices. 3. Monetary policy. I. Wood, Geoffrey
Edward. II. Institute of Economic Affairs (Great Britain)
HG221.M8164 1998
332.4—dc21   98–13454
                                                                        CIP

ISBN   978 1 85898 612 5 (cased)
       978 1 84720 673 2 (paperback)

Contents

v

Figures

Tables

Introduction

Geoffrey E. Wood

Every developed economy uses money, and money pervades every aspect of
the economy. The contributions to this volume examine only a limited number
of the numerous aspects of money's role, but they are the most basic ones.
They deal with what money is; the relationship between money and prices; the
importance of price stability; the relationship between monetary policy and
the behaviour of the economy; the relationship between money and output;
the relationship between money and interest rates; developing operational
guidelines for the conduct of monetary policy; and with aspects of the role
of a central bank. This brief introduction puts the eight chapters in context,
touches on a few matters that they do not cover, and concludes by setting out
their main points.[1]

WHAT IS MONEY?

In Chapter 1, Allan Meltzer addresses the fundamental issue of what money is
and what it does in an economy. The question, 'What is money?', also arises in
another, very important albeit less fundamental, sense. This is the operational
definition of money from the point of view of someone either carrying out or
interpreting monetary policy. Partly this latter involves distinguishing between
different statistical measures of the money supply: M0 (notes and coin plus
bankers' balances at the central bank) and M1 (M0 + current accounts), for
example. It also, however, involves distinguishing between money and credit.

Monetary economics is concerned with the determinants of levels and rates of
change of *nominal variables*, and with the influence of these nominal variables
on real variables. The price level is a nominal variable, as is its rate of change,
the inflation rate. What is credit? Credit is the granting of a loan from a creditor
(that is, the lender) to a debtor (the borrower). Note that before there can be
credit there must be *both* a lender and a borrower. Hence the amount of credit
extended by a loan must exactly equal the amount of debt – negative credit
– incurred by the borrower. If both parties to the transaction are considered,
the *net* amount of credit is zero. Hence any measure of 'credit outstanding' in
an economy must be zero, unless it is explicitly a measure of the net credit

position of a *part* of the economy. It is meaningful, in other words, to talk of the net credit or debit position of, for example, households, but only that of the economy as a whole when international transactions are considered. Many different measures of credit can be constructed by partitioning the economy in different ways. Each measure, if it is useful at all, is useful for a particular purpose. That purpose, however, can *never* be to measure the total of credit. Hence credit and money are quite different.

This does not mean that credit, and the associated financial markets in which it is traded, are unimportant for monetary economics. Credit is important in that it can allow an increased number of transactions to be carried out with the same quantity of money. Credit cards do this; they let individuals get by with a smaller amount of cash but still make the same number of purchases. Credit markets, markets in borrowing and lending, are the markets in which consumption and savings decisions interact. These are *real* decisions, and the consequences for them of monetary actions can be important. But that said, money and credit are different in kind; they do not lie along some smooth continuum on which the placing of divisions is arbitrary.

MONEY AND INTEREST RATES

Any interest rate we see quoted[2] is what is called a nominal interest rate. That is, it tells how many pounds (for example) one will get if one buys £100 of the asset and holds it for some period, usually a year. Such interest rates have two components: a real return and a compensation for inflation. A nominal interest rate equals the real rate of interest plus the expected rate of change of prices over the life of the asset. To see why this is so, consider what is implied if, for example, expected inflation rises but nominal interest rates do not. The rate of return lenders receive has thus fallen; their investment will let them buy less at the end of the year than it would have before. If borrowers and lenders were content with their transactions before, they will not be now; borrowers will wish to borrow more, lenders to lend less. Hence nominal interest rates will rise until real rates are the same as before. That of course describes the final, equilibrium, result. The transition to that can be – and almost invariably is – extremely complicated, and is an important aspect of the interaction between monetary and real variables.[3] This process is set out in more detail by Professor Robert Rasche in Chapter 2.

THE QUANTITY THEORY OF MONEY

The quantity theory of money is one of the oldest-established theories in economics. It states that (for example) in a gold standard world a doubling of the quantity of gold would eventually produce only a doubling in prices measured in units of gold. Hence, in turn, long-lasting growth in the quantity of gold would produce long-lasting growth in the price level: that is, inflation.

This proposition is clearly related to what is known as monetarism. Both quantity theorists and monetarists would accept that money growth, in excess of the growth of income, will produce inflation, and that, in addition, such money growth will have at most a temporary stimulative effect on output. Is there then any difference between quantity theorists and monetarists? Samuel Brittan has written, 'The quantity theory is basically less mechanistic than monetarism.' (Financial Times, 15 June 1995). That captures the essence of the matter. Quantity theorists and monetarists agree on the conclusions. But quantity theorists lay particular stress on long-run relations, while monetarists tend (though certainly not exclusively) to rely on econometric examination of smaller data sets, and to be less relaxed about temporary deviations from the long-run relations.[4]

OPEN AND CLOSED ECONOMIES

None of the present authors deals explicitly with the different impact of money in open and closed economies (although there is implicit analysis of the issue by Forrest Capie in Chapter 2). It is therefore worthwhile spending a little time on the subject, as ignoring the distinction often has led to confusion.

In a closed economy – one with no net monetary flows between itself and the rest of the world – a monetary expansion will lead, as described by the quantity theory, to a roughly proportionate rise in prices. The economy can be closed for this purpose by somehow cutting it off from the rest of the world, or by the less drastic expedient of having a freely floating exchange rate. The latter would ensure that any attempt to produce a net flow of the country's currency abroad would result simply in a depreciation of the currency on the foreign exchanges, as sales of it increased.

But in an open economy – where net money flows are possible – the result is different. Such an economy is open to trade, and has a pegged exchange rate. The behaviour of the money supply in that economy is then determined by the country in a fixed exchange rate system whose monetary policy every other country follows. In other words, money matters and the quantity theory holds in open and closed economies; but only in closed economies (and the monetary leader in a group of open economies) are monetary conditions under domestic control. The ERM is a good example. Countries joining it gave up control of their monetary conditions. But they did so, not because money would then cease to affect prices, but because money would continue to affect prices, and the monetary policy of Germany, the lead country in the system, was thought to be superior to their own.

THE CONTRIBUTIONS

Having set out the context, it is now possible to conclude with a few words on the contributions in this volume. In Chapter 1, Allan Meltzer explains what money is – primarily a medium of exchange – and shows how the use of a medium of exchange brings both benefits and costs to society. He emphasizes that the use of a medium of exchange brings benefits in the form of lower costs: it 'lowers costs of acquiring information by shifting attention to the properties of the asset [that is, the medium of exchange] and away from personal attributes such as creditworthiness of the buyer'. The same information is required for every transaction; there is no need to gather information every time one transacts. There are of course costs of using money – to the individual, risk of loss or theft, to society, risk of inflation or monetarily induced cyclical instability. The benefits must, however, be considerable; for, as Allan Meltzer notes, money continues to be used even in periods of very rapid inflation. The following quotation encapsulates his argument and conclusions: 'Resources allocated to search and to maintaining market information can be reallocated once money is used as a medium of exchange. Trade and the market system expand' (p. 18).

In Chapter 2, Forrest Capie examines the relationship between money and prices. It is the contribution of a quantity theorist. Long runs of data are examined, from both recent periods and as far back as the Roman Empire. The robustness of the relationship between money growth and prices stands out regardless of the nature of the society, its level of development, what kinds of goods it produces and whether inflation is fast or slow. Capie also shows how monetary expansion spilled over from one country to others when exchange rates were fixed, but was contained within a country's borders by exchange rate flexibility. This chapter is rich in historical data and in conclusions drawn from these data, and is a lucid demonstration of the enduring and all-pervasive validity of the quantity theory.

But so what? Does inflation matter? Anna Schwartz answers this question. Briefly, inflation disturbs all markets. It makes it more likely that banks will fail, with the widespread economic damage that follows: 'if inflation and price instability prevail, so also will financial instability'. She argues compellingly that many conventional estimates of the cost of inflation, by omitting the adverse consequences for financial stability, greatly understate the costs for the real economy. Chapter 3 is a forceful refutation of the claim that a little inflation does no harm.

Michael Bordo assesses the relationship between money supply regime and economic performance. His definition of monetary regime is a most useful one: 'we define a monetary regime as a set of monetary arrangements and institutions accompanied by a set of expectations – expectations by the public with respect to policy makers' actions and expectations by policy makers about the public's reaction to their actions' (p. 42). Bordo contrasts the performance of regimes based on convertibility into a precious metal with that of inconvertible – unbacked paper money – systems. He examines, too, both domestic and international aspects of the regime, and ranges widely across countries and through time. Price-level performance was clearly better under convertibility. The conclusions for real performance are not so clear, but he argues that, on balance, this superior price-level performance was not bought at the price of greater real instability.

It is clear, then, what the objective of monetary policy ought to be – price stability. But how to achieve it? Numerous approaches have been tried. Currently inflation targets are fashionable. An increasing number of countries, including Britain, have announced that the objective of monetary policy is to keep inflation within a low and pre-announced range. That is an admirable statement of the objective. But does it help us to get there? In 1960, Milton Friedman pointed out a problem with inflation targets. His argument can be summarized as follows.

The central bank does not and cannot control the price level. It *can* control the stock of money. This distinction is important because, while the stock of money is 'systematically related to the price level *on the average*' (emphasis in original), the short-run relationship is variable, especially for mild movements, and further, the lags between money and inflation are highly variable. The evidence, he wrote, 'is sufficient to pin the *average* lead within a narrow range' (*A Program for Monetary Stability*, Fordham University Press, p. 88). But, he went on, 'it is the highly variable behavior for the individual episode with which policy must be concerned' (ibid.).

This raises a serious problem with regard to inflation targeting and one not invalidated by the experience to date of inflation-targeting economies. Their experience is far too short for success to be claimed. This is where Bennett McCallum's chapter comes in. McCallum reviews the various ways in which a central bank's monetary policy actions can be guided. He concludes, after a most careful and judicious weighing of evidence, that adjusting monetary policy to keep money terms national income growing within a small and steady range is both desirable and feasible. He thus solves the problem of how to achieve what every other chapter in this volume has shown to be not merely desirable, but rather the very heart of a satisfactory monetary policy: stable and very low inflation, at a rate equivalent for all practical purposes to price stability.

Chapter 6 traces the impact of a monetary shock from its first effect on interest rates through to its final conclusion, and examines the extent to which this theoretical exposition conforms with some data. This analysis links particularly with two other chapters in the volume. In the finding that money ultimately does not affect real interest rates, it is consistent with the results surveyed in Capie's study of money and prices. It also shows the great complexity of the short-run, transitional, relationship and thus further illuminates the complexity of another short-run relationship, that between money and output, discussed by Robert Rasche in Chapter 7. This chapter by Rasche provides both a lesson in economics and a lesson in the history of economic thought. It proceeds chronologically, from the period in the late 1940s and early 1950s, when it was unhesitatingly accepted that money would stimulate real output without price-level effects, through the years when it was believed that money could permanently raise output but at the cost of permanently raising inflation, to the present situation, where it is accepted that money cannot affect output permanently, but that it may, perhaps, have temporary effects. Robert Rasche explains with particular lucidity why the present state of knowledge about the short-run effects is so uncertain, and suggests how research on this topic may proceed in the future.

The dangers of inflation have been pointed out in this introduction, and are discussed in more than one chapter. It should not be forgotten that, just as the monetary expansions which produce inflation should be avoided, so should monetary contractions below the monetary conditions appropriate for price stability. For sharp monetary contractions produce recession; indeed, such a contraction was responsible for the Great Depression in the United States.[5] How are such events to be avoided? An important aspect of doing so is the preservation of a stable banking system. If banks collapse, a monetary squeeze is imposed on the economy as bank deposits are wiped out. The preservation of banking stability is discussed by Charles Calomiris in Chapter 8 which puts the subject in its historical context by examining first how the role of government in the banking system gradually expanded, not so much by design as by a series of ad hoc responses to one-off shocks.[6] Before the 1930s, the main institutions which protected banks were other banks. That changed in the USA in the 1930s, and other countries followed in the post-World War II period.

After some years of stability, the financial system was again troubled by shocks in the 1980s. The initial response was to increase protection still further. But then, and this is the analysis developed in Chapter 8, it started to be realized that the 'protecting' devices exacerbated the problem. This was probably recognized first in the USA, but, as the chapter shows, was fairly soon afterwards admitted in several other countries as well. Having set out that historical background, Professor Calomiris then applies economic analysis to show how banking stability can be preserved. In doing so, he uses microeconomics (microeconomics and macroeconomics are often treated as almost separate subjects, but they are not).

As Calomiris points out, his proposals have not yet been universally accepted or adopted. But, as he also points out, countries which have adopted them have so far achieved the objectives they sought. This fascinating chapter blends theory, institutions and history, and also brings us right up to date with current economic policy problems.

CONCLUDING OVERVIEW

The contributions in this volume have certainly not reviewed every aspect of monetary economics, but they do deal in their range of topics with the very essence and core of monetary economics – what money does for us, why price stability is vital and, as important though often neglected, how to achieve the highly desirable objectives of price stability and stability of the banking system. They also guide and, it is hoped, stimulate, the reader towards further and more detailed study of the subject.

NOTES

1. The reader seeking a more lengthy overview of the main contents and conclusions of monetary economics could not do better than read Chapters 1 and 2 of *Monetary Economics* by Bennett T. McCallum (London: Collier Macmillan, 1984).
2. With the partial and complex exceptions of the interest rate on British government indexed bonds.
3. A terse but extremely lucid exposion of it can be found in *Monetary Trends in the US and the UK*, by Milton Friedman and Anna J. Schwartz (Chicago: University of Chicago Press, 1982), pp. 477–500. Discussion of the distinction between real and nominal interest rates also reveals how inflation acts as a tax. The classic source here is 'The Welfare Cost of Inflationary Finance', by Martin J. Bailey (*Journal of Political Economy*, 1956, **LXIV**, (23), April, 93–110).
4. The quantity theory and its connections with monetarism are discussed in a recent collection of essays, *The Quantity Theory of Money: From Locke to Keynes to Friedman*, by M. Blaug *et al.*, (Aldershot: Edward Elgar, 1995).
5. This dramatic episode in monetary economics is discussed in Chapter 3 of *A Monetary History of the United States*, by Milton Friedman and Anna J. Schwartz (Princeton: Princeton University Press, for NBER, 1963).
6. Many of Professor Calomiris' examples (though not all) are drawn from the USA, but these are illustrations of problems which apply in every banking system.

1.   What is money?

Allan H. Meltzer

Money is the medium of exchange. This simple statement answers the question: What is money? But the answer merely shifts attention to a different set of questions. What is a medium of exchange? Why is it used? What benefits or costs accrue to individuals and society from the use of money?

Attempts to answer these questions have introduced 'motives' for holding or using money, legal restrictions, or assumed some difficult-to-define services provided by money, for example liquidity. Motives include the transactions and precautionary reasons for holding money. Money is used in transactions or to reduce costs of bearing uncertainty about the timing of future receipts or payments. The transactions and precautionary motives suggest reasons why money is used or held, but they do not explain why the same small group of assets is used repetitively for this purpose. Why are many transactions settled by use of a medium of exchange? Why do people use money instead of other assets to adjust for differences in the timing of receipts and payments?

Money is a nominal stock with a nominal price of unity; a dollar is a dollar, and a pound is a pound. The real value of a unit of money is $1/p$ where p is some measure of the cost of a basket of goods and services such as the consumer or retail price index. As p rises, each unit of money buys fewer real goods and services. The real value of a unit of money falls and, in periods of high inflation, the real value of money falls rapidly. The cost of holding money rises with the price level. The longer money is held, the less each unit is worth. People use substitutes for money to avoid the costs of holding money. Yet money continued to be used even in the famous German hyperinflation of the 1920s, in other hyperinflations at that time and, more recently, in the high inflations experienced in Argentina, Bolivia, Brazil, Chile and Israel during the 1980s.

The continued use of money when prices rise at a rate of 100, 500 or 1000 per cent per year or more suggests how costly it is to replace existing money with new money. Barter as an alternative to money is a very costly and cumbersome procedure. Often multiple transactions – lengthy transaction

* Most of this essay is based on Karl Brunner and Allan H. Meltzer, 'The Uses of Money: Money in the Theory of an Exchange Economy', *American Economic Review*, 1971, **61** (December), 784–805.

chains – are required to exchange the good or service offered for the good or service desired. The German inflation that followed World War II provides a case study. The US army estimated that barter was used in one-third to one-half of all business transactions in the US and British zones of Germany. Most of the remaining transactions were settled in rapidly depreciating German money. Money continued to be used as a medium of exchange despite the high inflation rate.

In Latin American or Eastern European countries that have experienced high inflation rates in the recent past, prices are often quoted in US dollars and many transactions are settled in dollars. The dollar is used as a unit of account particularly for purchases and sales of houses, land and other durable assets. Often this use persists long after inflation rates have been reduced. Tourists find hotel rental rates quoted in dollars and many prices indexed to the dollar. The dollar is also used as a medium of exchange in these countries. A present-day traveller in Russia, much of Eastern Europe and large parts of Latin America will have no difficulty offering payment in dollars.

People in these countries do not choose the dollar as a unit of account or medium of exchange because it has the lowest rate of inflation. Inflation rates in Germany and Japan have been lower for many years past. The dollar is used because it is widely recognized by both sellers and buyers. The use of the dollar in these countries suggests the importance of information in the choice of money

MONEY IN ECONOMIC THEORY

Standard economic theory has difficulty explaining the use of money. Transactions take place in a central market at announced prices. By assumption all markets clear, and all transactions are settled at once. By holding money, transactors pay a cost; they could have more goods and services if they did not hold money. There are no offsetting benefits to compensate for this cost.

To explain the ubiquitous use of money, economists depart from the standard model most often by introducing lack of synchronization of payments. Money is said to bridge the gap between receipts and payments. Receipts are assumed to be made weekly or monthly, while spending and payments are continuous. People receive income in the form of money, pay out money to purchase goods and services, and hold the unspent balance as either money or some short-term asset. Transaction costs are assumed to be high enough to induce people to hold some (low- or) non-interest bearing money instead of interest-yielding Treasury bills or other short-term assets.

Lack of synchronization does not imply that money is used or held. If there were no costs of information, transactors could issue verbal promises to pay. Later, when income is received, they could discharge the debt. This introduces credit – promises to pay – to solve the synchronization problem. Transactions could differ in time and place. If there were no uncertainty and no cost of acquiring information, everyone would know with certainty the income stream of any buyer, as well as everyone's payments, liabilities, assets and wealth position. Default risk is zero under the posited conditions, so the only cost to issuing credit is the time value of payments. Credit is used in developed economies to defer payment of purchases. Debts are discharged by paying money, not by the exchange of goods as in a barter-credit economy that has no money. A small number of assets serves as the means of payment to settle credit transactions and to pay for goods, services and assets at time of purchase.

To explain the use of money – a small number of assets that serve as a medium of exchange – two additional postulates must be introduced into economic theory. The first postulate makes the marginal cost of acquiring information, measured in units of consumption sacrificed, depend on the goods or services selected for use in exchange. The second postulate says that the marginal cost of acquiring information about the properties of any asset falls as the frequency of use within a social group increases. These postulates are necessary and sufficient to establish the use of a medium of exchange. They emphasize the uneven distribution of information that makes the use of a common medium of exchange useful and productive for transactions.

The usefulness of a medium of exchange and the fact that money is a stock imply that money is held. Hence money is a store of value as well as a medium of exchange. However, money is relatively unimportant as a store of value. In economies with developed financial markets, the stock of money is a small fraction of wealth, as little as 2 per cent of the consolidated wealth of an economy.

THE SERVICES OF MONEY TO INDIVIDUAL TRANSACTORS

The traditional explanation of money is that money avoids the inconvenience of barter. Barter, it is said, involves the double coincidence of wants; each transactor must desire to trade what he owns for what the other transactor has. Barter-credit eliminates the double coincidence problem without introducing money. But barter-credit is rare. The use of a medium of exchange brings advantages that make this social arrangement a dominant arrangement for individuals and for society.

The use of money lowers costs of acquiring information by shifting attention to the properties of the asset and away from personal attributes such as creditworthiness of the buyer, his reputation, wealth or income. The buyer gains because it is less costly to make purchases; the seller gains for the same reason. Information costs are lower. Since purchasing becomes less costly, more purchases are made. Trade expands.

Transactions with a medium of exchange can be anonymous. The buyer who pays currency to acquire goods or services does not have to verify or reveal information to the seller. The seller only has to establish that the money offered by the buyer is genuine, not counterfeit. The ability to recognize an asset used as medium of exchange increases with the frequency of use, as the second postulate specifies.

Use of precious metals, such as gold and silver, as means of payment spread in the Middle Ages. Gold or silver could be weighed to verify the value offered in exchange. Knowledge of the value of the means of payment was much easier to obtain and verify than knowledge of the value of randomly selected commodities or the wealth and honesty of a buyer or the value of his promise to pay. Transaction chains narrowed to a few objects. Eventually gold and silver became the dominant mediums of exchange for international transactions, the international money of that era and many later eras. Use of these precious metals became common in domestic transactions also.

Textbooks invariably note that divisibility, portability and durability are among the properties of money. These generalizations are not without exception. Shells and rocks have been used as money. In wartime German prison camps, cigarettes were used as money. As these examples illustrate, information about the properties of an asset and knowledge that others have the same information are common to all moneys, even those that are not divisible, portable or durable.

Once knowledge spreads that an object is generally used in settlement of debts and payment for goods and services, it becomes money – the medium of exchange. The medium of exchange may acquire other attributes. The government may make money legal tender for paying taxes and other pecuniary obligations owed to government. Prices may be quoted in units of the medium of exchange; money used as a medium of exchange may also be used as a unit of account.

There is no necessity that the medium of exchange, the unit of account and legal tender be the same. The use of the dollar as medium of exchange in Russia, Latin America and elsewhere results from private decisions. Rarely is the dollar designated as legal tender in foreign countries. Likewise there are many historical examples of separate units of account used to designate value. The British guinea is a well-known historical example. Money prices could be quoted in guineas though payments were made in pounds. A current example, referred to earlier, is the use of dollar prices for real property and durables in countries with a history of high inflation. Payment may be made in dollars or in the current local currency equivalent. The ECU used in the European Monetary System is another example of a modern unit of account that is not a medium of exchange.

The use of money as a unit of account reduces information costs for transactors. Without a unit of account, any transactor must know the bilateral exchange value of each commodity for every other commodity. If there are n commodities, there are at least $(n(n-1))/2$ separate values. The number of bilateral exchange ratios (prices) rises quickly. With $n = 100$ commodities, there are at least 4950 prices to know. At $n = 500$, the number is 124 750, and with 1000 commodities there are at least 499 500 prices. Without a unit of account, trade would be limited by costs of information. Traders would not know the value of items offered in exchange. Use of a unit of account to express value reduces the number of prices from $(n(n-1))/(2)$ to n. This reduction in costs of information encourages the expansion of trade.

After a physical object such as a metal becomes money, resources can be saved by issuing claims against the metal. Goldsmiths in the Middle Ages stored gold and precious metals to protect the owners from theft or loss. At first the goldsmiths provided safekeeping. Later they learned that there was a low probability that all the gold would be claimed at once. The goldsmiths could profit by issuing paper claims to the gold in their vaults in excess of the value of the gold. Thus goldsmiths became bankers, and paper claims to gold circulated in place of gold. Eventually paper currency became not just a claim to gold but a fiat money with no backing.

The low cost of producing paper currency is a benefit to society if an effective principle is used to limit the amount issued. Without such limitation, overproduction of currency leads to inflation that destroys the value of currency, money and all nominal values. For the individual, there are other costs to using currency. Risk of loss and robbery are not negligible. The anonymity that makes currency valuable as a medium of exchange makes it difficult to identify or claim lost or stolen currency.

Demand deposits or cheques are also used to settle transactions. Unlike the case of currency, anonymity is no longer possible. The seller requires information about the buyer. Payment by cheque is generally restricted to people who can establish credit with the seller or with an intermediary who issues a credit card. Electronic systems of verification have reduced the costs of information about users of credit cards, encouraging their use. A credit card substitutes for money at the time of purchase, but credit transactions are settled by the payment of money, typically by using chequing deposits. Money serves as the means of payment in transactions of this kind by discharging the debt incurred when using a credit card.

To analyse the medium of exchange function more fully, consider a transactor who has an initial endowment of resources including his own labour time and some information about exchange ratios and qualities of commodities. He has several alternative ways of transforming his initial endowment into a preferred bundle. As in standard price theory, he can use his endowment for production, consumption or exchange. In addition, he has two options that are neglected in traditional price theory. First, he can use resources to increase his information about the qualities of goods and opportunities for exchange. If the transactor uses resources in this way, he invests in information. Second, he can engage in indirect or roundabout methods of exchange, accepting goods with low marginal cost of acquiring information, transferring and storing, then exchanging these goods for others until he obtains an optimal bundle. The resources allocated to the exchange process are the (real) costs of transacting or exchanging and are, of course, distinct from the resources exchanged.

Under conditions of uncertainty about the quality of goods offered in exchange and about prevailing market opportunities, the costs of acquiring information and exchanging are neither zero nor identical for every good or service. The first postulate, introduced above, recognizes that the marginal cost of the resources the transactor uses to acquire information or to carry out transactions is the amount of consumption or endowment sacrificed. This marginal cost depends on the goods or services he selects (or about which he chooses to acquire information) and is different for different goods.

By choosing a sequence of transactions – a transaction chain – involving assets with low marginal cost of information, a transactor can lower the marginal cost of exchanging. He incurs transfer and carrying costs and uses existing information about the qualities of particular goods instead of investing resources to acquire information about other goods or other trading arrangements. However transfer costs increase with the length of the transaction chain, encouraging the rational transactor to compare the marginal cost of acquiring information with the marginal cost of rearranging the transaction chain and with the benefits obtained from these and alternative uses of resources.

The first postulate makes the marginal cost of acquiring information depend on the good or service selected to be received in exchange. This choice allows the transactor to reduce the resource cost of acquiring a preferred set of commodities by substituting knowledge about transaction arrangements for investment in information about market conditions and the qualities of goods offered in exchange. Cost reduction occurs in two ways. First, detailed information about market conditions such as location and identification of transactors, the quality and type of commodity bundles they hold and the exchange ratios at which they trade probably decays more rapidly than knowledge about optimal transaction chains. Second, as the use of an asset in exchange increases, the transactor learns more about the asset's properties. With growing use of particular transaction chains and improved knowledge of the properties of the assets exchanged, uncertainty about the asset's properties declines. Less investment in information is required to maintain the value of information about desirable transaction chains. Thus the first postulate ensures that the choice of transaction chain and of the assets used in exchange is neither random nor determined solely by the exchange: that is, by the initial and terminal commodity bundles with which trade begins and ends.

The second postulate states (1) that the marginal cost of acquiring information does not vary randomly within a social group and (2) that the marginal cost declines as the frequency with which an asset is used increases. Transactors can acquire information about a particular subset of the available assets at comparatively low marginal cost once these assets are used frequently. Technical properties such as portability, divisibility and durability influence the choice.

The second postulate implies that the transaction chains of the numerous participants in the market process exhibit some common properties. The repetitive use of a relatively small number of transaction chains by the members of a social group further reduces the marginal cost to each transactor of acquiring information about the assets most frequently used. The lower costs of acquiring information and transacting induce further clustering and the convergence of individuals' chains towards a common pattern.

There are many stages of development between double-coincidence barter and a fully monetary economy. At some stage a few assets are used with dominant frequency in transactions. Money as a medium of exchange, as a transaction-dominating asset, results from the opportunities offered by the distribution of incomplete information and the search by potential transactors to develop transaction chains that save resources.

The analysis also explains the emergence of specialized trading functions such as brokerage and other market arrangements. They develop from the conditions that shape the (social) convergence to a dominant medium of exchange. Where information is complete and both information and readjustment are costless, specialization of trading functions yields no economic advantages and has no utility. Where information and readjustment are not free, the situation changes. Specialized services lower the costs of acquiring information and trading by providing more complete information about the range of qualities and market conditions. With a smaller investment of resources a transactor acquires the same information, and more resources can be used for consumption or trade.

THE SOCIAL SERVICES OF MONEY

For individuals, money is a substitute for investment in information and labour or time allocated to search. By using money, individuals reduce the amount of information they must acquire, process and store, and they reduce the number of transactions in which they engage to exchange their initial endowments for desired baskets of goods. The use of money increases the welfare of each money user by reducing uncertainty and the length of transaction chains and by increasing expected wealth and time available for leisure. Whatever other services create a demand for the assets that serve as mediums of exchange, their use as mediums of exchange increases demand. Individuals find it advantageous to allocate part of their wealth to money.

What is true for individuals is in this case true for society. The convergence of optimal transaction arrangements generates an aggregate demand for the assets used as mediums of exchange. The increased demand to hold inventories of these assets (money) is independent of the previous uses of the assets and, of course, increases the (relative) prices of the assets. The average amount held in cash balances depends on the prices of the assets held, the prices of alternative assets and, thus, on the relation between net marginal productivity and marginal cost.

Once inventories of money are held, payments and receipts are no longer synchronized. Lack of synchronization, however, does not explain the use or holding of money any more than the holding of money explains the lack of synchronization. Both are a result of the superior productivity of indirect methods of exchange, the smaller resource cost of acquiring information and transacting in a monetary economy.

The use of money encourages the development of the market system by lowering the costs of acquiring information and transacting. With the expansion of the market, opportunities increase for professional middlemen and specialized traders to exploit the partial and incomplete distribution of information about particular commodities. Specialized traders substitute for a wider and more general distribution of information. The use of money also affects the intertemporal allocation of resources. Deferred payments, borrowing, credit and the payments system expand when a standardized asset with well-known properties becomes money for the particular group. The reason is that transactors become more willing to enter into contracts calling for deferred payment.

The magnitude of the net social productivity of money is not constant but varies with the degree of uncertainty about market conditions, including exchange ratios and the qualities of goods. Accelerated technological changes or innovations that change the qualities of goods and increase the number or types of goods raise the productivity of money. Large fluctuations in economic activity also raise costs of acquiring information and the productivity of money.

This analysis implies that the demand for mediums of exchange is higher in periods of rapid change than in periods of gradual or relatively steady change. The longer a period of steady, gradual change continues, the lower the productivity of money and the smaller the demand for assets that reduce costs of acquiring information by serving as mediums of exchange.

A stationary state or a world of steady growth are the limiting cases of economic theory. Tastes, technology, anticipations, population and types of product are either invariant or change in a known, fully anticipated way at a steady rate. The marginal cost of acquiring information falls and in the limit approaches zero. Transaction chains no longer differ by the saving of costs of acquiring information and differ only by the costs of transfer. The main condition leading to the selection of a small group of assets as money, and therefore the main source of the distinction between money and non-monetary assets, disappears in the stationary state or world of steady growth.

The introduction of money and its widespread use suggests that the gross gain to individuals and societies from using money is much larger than the saving in transaction costs emphasized in most textbooks. The latter are marginal benefits once money is used. The gross benefits include the saving in information costs. The use of money also introduces two social costs that partly offset the gross benefits. First is the risk of inflation or deflation. Individual prices can change in a non-monetary economy, but inflation – a maintained increase in the rate of price change – can only occur in a monetary economy. Second is the risk generated by business cycles. The use of money permits people to shift from purchases of commodities to money holding. Since all prices do not adjust instantly, this increased demand for money has real effects. Aggregate demand and output fall. Unanticipated reductions in the stock of money have similar effects on aggregate demand and output. Historically changes in the stock of money have been a major cause of cyclical fluctuations.

The size of the net social productivity of money depends on the assets selected as mediums of exchange. Once the community uses some assets as money, the private and social benefit can be increased by substituting claims against commodities for commodity money. Individuals gain from the use of substitutes for commodity money if the reduction of costs of acquiring information and transacting more than compensates for any increased variability of exchange ratios such as occurs in periods of inflation and deflation. There are potential net gains because the use of claims and fiat paper money reduces costs and resources used to make exchange in three main ways. First, paper money permits society to develop a fractional reserve money system and to produce the same nominal stock of money at lower resource cost. Second, the use of claims encourages the development of privately produced money and with it the development of the payments system. The cost of acquiring information about the qualities of paper money, whether produced by government or by private producers, is lowest if the paper money starts as a claim against commodity money. Historically, when information about the paper money becomes widespread, paper money has retained the property of general acceptability after the right to claim commodities has been removed. Third, paper money frequently lowers the resource cost of transfer and exchange. This somewhat less than general proposition recognizes that both costs and benefits are affected and that the size of the net benefit from the use of paper money depends on the prevailing monetary arrangements and the type of monetary policy followed.

Monetary history offers numerous examples of changes in monetary arrangements that reduced marginal costs of information or transfer for the assets used in optimal transaction chains. Subsidiary coinage is one of the earliest, and bank credit cards one of the most recent, steps extending the range and use of mediums of exchange by reducing these costs. Suppose, however, that paper money is not introduced by a central bank or government but emerges in response to the public's search for optimal transaction chains. Many different producers are induced to issue paper money as a claim against commodity money. The social benefit resulting from the use of lower cost money is partly offset by the higher cost individuals pay to acquire information. The legislation of 1844 in England and of the 1860s in the USA that reduced the number and types of notes in circulation by restricting the right to issue notes are examples of institutional changes that raised economic welfare by reducing costs of acquiring information. The requirement of par collection of cheques under the Federal Reserve Act is another example.

The analysis does not imply either that society converges to a single medium of exchange or that the productivity of money and the contribution of money to wealth is limited to a single monetary asset. Different types of assets – some privately, some publicly produced – typically appear in the transaction chains adopted within a group and in the transaction chains of a single transactor at different times. These differences in the choice of transaction chain reflect differences in marginal cost that depend on the type of transaction and the transactor's information. Even in highly developed economies with extensive monetary institutions, transactors can use specialized information to develop transaction arrangements that lower transfer costs by avoiding the use of money. Moreover sectors of an economy that develop specialized information about the properties of particular assets often find it useful to develop specialized mediums of exchange. An example is the use of deferred equity claims of various kinds in mergers and acquisitions. Skilled professionals use their knowledge and information to develop payment mechanisms that reduce taxes and other costs.

Our analysis suggests an extension of Gresham's law – cheap money drives out dear at fixed exchange rates – to the case of multiple mediums of exchange with variable or floating exchange rates. With floating exchange rates, stable monies drive out variable monies. Consequently government or private producers seeking to maintain the circulation of government and privately produced moneys have found it desirable to provide arrangements for exchange of one money for the other on demand. Typically they set the price of currency in demand deposits at unity and guarantee conversion.

CONCLUSION

The use of money remained puzzling as long as the theory of exchange was restricted to the case of perfect certainty, a world in which information about market prices and the qualities of goods and services is obtained at zero cost. Standard price theory eliminated the main reasons for the existence and use of money by confining choice to three options – production, consumption and exchange – and setting costs of acquiring information about exchange opportunities and qualities of goods to zero. With costs of executing transactions zero and information a free good, there are no costs of shopping to ensure that exchanges take place at the most favourable prices and no benefits from reducing the resource cost of executing transactions and eliminating cross-hauling of commodities. Any asset is just as usable as any other for executing transactions and discharging obligations. As a result, attempts to explain the use of money generally accept some arrangements that accompany the use of money, such as lack of synchronization, as an explanation of the existence of money.

The existence of money ceases to be a puzzle once we recognize differences in costs of acquiring information about market arrangements, relative prices or exchange ratios. Individuals search for those sequences of transactions, called transaction chains, that minimize the cost of acquiring information and transacting. The use of assets with peculiar technical properties and low marginal cost of acquiring information reduces these costs. Money is such an asset, and the private and social productivity of money are a direct consequence of the saving in resources that the use of money permits and of the extension of the market system that occurs because of the reduction in the cost of making exchanges.

Money is a substitute for the specialized market skills that are part of a transactor's stock of knowledge or 'human wealth'. Resources allocated to search and to maintaining market information can be reallocated once money is used as a medium of exchange. Trade and the market system expand, and the economy becomes increasingly monetized. More and better quality information becomes available with the expansion of the market and the opportunities for division of labour that lead to the development of professional transactors such as brokers and specialists. The use of a unit of account further reduces the cost of making exchanges.

The recognition of the central role of money as a medium of exchange does not imply that the collection of assets that serves as medium of exchange is most appropriate for explaining movements of the general price level. A definition embracing a larger collection of assets is appropriate if there are close substitutes for the medium of exchange on the supply size. In this case, slight changes in relative prices reallocate output between the medium of exchange and other assets, so the collection of assets most useful for explaining changes in the general price level differs from the assets that serve as medium of exchange. However, even if evidence suggests that a broader collection is justified empirically and the term 'money' is used to refer to the broader collection, the significance of the medium of exchange function and its importance for explaining the productivity of a medium of exchange remains.

2. The long-run relationship between money and prices

Forrest. H. Capie

In the 1980s and 1990s there has been growing interest in, and discussion of, central bank independence. There has also been widespread agreement that some kind of independence is desirable. What lies behind this is a disappointment with price level performance in the period since World War II and a desire for price stability. There is an implicit acceptance that such stability comes from monetary stability, which in turn can best be achieved by removing the control of the money stock from the hands of politicians and placing it in the hands of a body independent of them. Politicians are readily seduced by the prospect of short-term electoral gains. As a consequence the money stock will frequently be expanded according to political goals and it will seldom be contracted. This produces an upward, if jagged, path in the money stock. Politicians therefore cannot be trusted, and independence is desirable.

The view that price stability goes with monetary stability derives from the very close association between money and prices over the long run. When the great sweep of history is considered, the fact is that, for most of the time, in the absence of paper money, there was little or no inflation. With the advent of paper money in the twentieth century that was to change dramatically. This chapter outlines what the association between money and prices has been and provides some specific examples of the association. It then discusses some of the more dramatic deviations from stability; finally it suggests how all this evidence fits the theory.

For most countries it is not possible to go very far back before data problems are encountered. Nevertheless much of the available information across several centuries, while not of a robust statistical kind, is still strongly suggestive. Long-run experience for many countries around the world has frequently followed the same pattern, in part a consequence of fixed exchange rate regimes prevailing. It follows, therefore, that where there are data for one or two important countries there can be some confidence that these are good proxies for many others; that is, that the price experience of large countries (large in the international trade sense) will be paralleled by many other countries which are closely associated with them.

PRICE HISTORY OF THE WORLD

If a graph were drawn of world prices from the beginning of time until the present day the truly striking feature would be the fact that the line would, apart from one or two isolated years, run close to the horizontal axis from the beginning of time until the twentieth century. It would then rise steeply, first in 1914–20 and then again in 1939–45, and continue after World War II on a steep upward trend. The same pattern would be found in modified form for most countries. For the fact is there was only the gentlest expansion of the money stock and of output, and almost no change in long-run prices for centuries at a time. There are no cases of a rapid expansion in the money stock that are not accompanied or followed by inflation, and neither are there any inflations that have not been paralleled or preceded by a rise in the money stock. This is true for as far back as we can go when speaking of something approaching a monetary economy.

A caution on the fragility of the data has to be given. For much of the time the data cannot be regarded as robust, but the patterns found, together with the available qualitative evidence, are suggestive, and support the basic hypothesis. Consider the decline of the Roman Empire in the course of the third century AD. The price data available suggest that there was a rise from a base of 100 in the year 200AD to 5000 by the end of the century, in other words a trend rate of growth of between 3 and 4 per cent per annum. (And there was, as might be expected, quite a lot of fluctuation around this trend.) Some accounts of the decline of the Roman Empire attribute that decline to debasement of the currency and the consequent inflation. Kent (1920, p. 47) claims that copper coin debasement was the main cause of the inflation, but he damages his case when he says that such debasement was equivalent to modern paper money expansion: 'Copper coins could very easily be manufactured and numismatists testify that the coins of the fourth century often bear signs of hasty and careless minting ... [this] was just as effective as our modern printing presses.' It may be significant that Kent was writing in 1920, before most of the really wild expansions in paper money had taken place. It is not believable that sufficient coins could either be minted or carried around to produce the rates of inflation that have been found in the twentieth century. In short, the kind of monetary expansion that was possible in Rome was consistent with the kind of inflation that they experienced, and equally could not lead to the kind of inflations found in the twentieth century.

While more is being discovered about the period once called the Dark Ages, following the fall of Rome and stretching from the fifth century until the beginning of the Middle Ages, there is still a dearth of data. It is not until the fourteenth century that price data begin to become more available. In the period that is known as the high Middle Ages there were several longish swings in prices. These can to some extent be accounted for by the ups and downs in population movements. Population growth speeded and slowed as a result of many factors (though at this time it was still constrained by the Malthusian trap[2]) but with a relatively fixed money stock the effects of the population movements were reflected in prices[3]. It must be remembered that it is the general price level that we are interested in and not relative prices. When population pressure was high some prices such as, say, those of grain would have been driven up while some others would have fallen. It would therefore be incautious, to put it at its mildest, to use grain prices as an indication of the general price level. In addition to population movements, on occasions there were some conscious monetary manipulations, the most common of which were the debasements carried out by the Crown.

By the sixteenth century the English experiments with money incidentally resulted in improved data. Sixteenth-century Europe is also well known as a period of high inflation. It was a time when gold and silver bullion were flowing in from the New World. Data deficiencies prevent any rigorous test, though the mere fact of the relatively steady increase in money being paralleled by a relatively steady increase in prices is highly suggestive; but it would be unwise to rule out the possibility that other factors had some role to play. In England prices rose by about 350 per cent over the 150 years from 1510 to 1660, an annual average rate of between 2 and 3 per cent. That of course is the period during which there were also considerable debasements of the coinage (and some restorations), though these debasements can be picked out as independent experiences.

Across the sixteenth and seventeenth centuries the experience in France was broadly similar to that in England. In Spain, where most of the metals arrived from the New World, prices rose faster than, and in advance of, those in the rest of Europe. In Andalusia, the actual point of entry for the bullion, price rises came first and were also the most rapid. In the second half of the sixteenth century prices there rose by 500 per cent, an annual rate of around 8 per cent. It is not possible to be sufficiently confident about the movements in output over this period to draw precise conclusions. However the very fact of these New World inflows of silver and gold being followed by rates of inflation which are broadly in line with what might be expected, given what we know in a qualitative fashion about output[4], certainly leaves this open to the interpretation that we have here further confirmation of the close long-run relationship between money and prices.

Other things were happening, of course, and other explanations have been offered. A principal objection to the monetary explanation has been that there is no demonstration that the money which indubitably flowed into Spain then flowed around the rest of Europe. For example, to take a typical case, England must have had a favourable balance of trade over a long period for the bullion to flow in. And yet a variety of investigations has not found the evidence for that. But these studies are very far from conclusive. They are generally based on our knowledge of isolated years or areas, for example of wool exports, or on trade data from one particular port. There are many counterarguments and the onus of proof would seem rather to rest with those who doubt the flow of specie from Spain to the rest of Europe. After all, the most likely occurrence would be that the new money in Spain bid up their prices and made foreign goods more attractive, that Spain then ran current account deficits and exported bullion and that in turn spread across the continent. In this respect it is surely suggestive that the highest price rises were found at the point of entry of the metal and that the rises in the rest of Europe followed.

Returning to the experience of England, the major English debasement occurred within this period of New World influx and that complicates the story at some points. In 1551, silver coin which had been debased by Henry VIII was recoined. Estimates of the money supply suggest that this resulted in a decline of the money stock of around 50 per cent. And yet there does not appear to have been a corresponding fall in prices. Over the next decade there was a growth in the money supply of about 20 per cent and in 1560 a further recoinage was carried out. Again neither the increase in money nor the sharp decrease seem to be reflected in price changes. This has led Schwartz to conclude that this is one period where price data do not reflect the behaviour of the money stock per unit of output. Schwartz does point out that the data deficiencies may well explain the differences, but there is an additional explanation. There was a serious outbreak of influenza in the 1550s, so serious that, by some estimates, it killed about 20 per cent of England's population. Not everyone accepts these estimates, but if anything close to that were true, and given that in addition there must have been extensive illness accompanying the epidemic that would have precluded work for long periods, the implications for output must be considered severe. Thus it could be that the collapse in the money stock consequent upon the recoinage was followed by a collapse in output, or was at least roughly contemporaneous with it. This would explain the lack of corresponding price movement. In other words it could be that the decline in the money stock from the recoinage was followed by a decline in output arising from the influenza epidemic and that prices stayed roughly constant. Then, to jump forward to the seventeenth century, following the cessation of the flow of new metals into Europe prices stopped rising.

To continue with the long sweep of the historical record, from around the middle of the seventeenth century until late in the eighteenth prices were generally flat, or perhaps on a gentle upward trend. There were two episodes of extreme inflation, to which we will return later, but they were brief and stand out in the flat trend. At the end of the eighteenth century and beginning of the nineteenth century, in the Napoleonic wars with the temporary abandonment of a metallic standard, further rapid monetary expansion took place, followed by price inflation. For example, in England at this time, over a period of about 25 years during much of which the pound was not convertible into gold, the best estimates of the excess monetary expansion (that is, expansion in excess of the growth of output) suggest it was of a similar order to the price inflation – a trend rate of roughly 3 per cent per annum.

A return to the gold standard (or to a bimetallic standard, one based on two metals, invariably gold and silver) in the 1820s resulted in prices returning to their previous pattern and continuing to be relatively stable across the nineteenth century. In Britain, prices in 1914 were broadly comparable to what they had been in 1821 (in so far as such long-period comparisons can be made given the changing nature of products and hence the difficulty of constructing satifactory price indices). There were sharp cyclical movements and some interesting secular swings around this trend. An example of the latter was that, towards the end of the century, in the period 1873–96, prices fell on trend; then, from 1896 to 1914, they rose so that the 1914 point was very close to that of 1873. The most convincing explanation for the fall is the contraction in the money stock relative to expanding real income, a result of the shortage of gold in the world economy which in turn was a consequence of the increasing number of countries which adopted the gold standard and held quantities of gold in their reserves. In Britain, in the price downswing of 1873–96, the money stock grew by 33 per cent. But real output in the period grew by 53 per cent. The respective annual growth rates were 1.3 per cent and 1.9 per cent. In other words there was a deficiency in the growth of money in relation to output, and prices fell. By contrast, in the upswing of 1896–1914, the money stock grew by 40 per cent and real output by 36 per cent. The respective annual growth rates were 2.0 per cent and 1.8 per cent, and so a slight excess monetary growth in relation to output went with gently rising prices.

THE USA AND THE UK

So much for a superficial look at the long run of price history. There are several important countries for which more intensive investigations of the relationship between money and prices have been made over the last one hundred years or so, again in so far as data allow. But there are two in particular in which there has been specific examination of the long-run relationship between the key monetary variables, the subject of this chapter. They are the USA and the UK in the work of Friedman and Schwartz (1982). What cannot be stressed too much about this truly monumental study is that it does not rely on any one technique but is instead a wide-ranging examination of all manner of evidence, derived from economic theory, statistics and history. There will always be questions raised over what is current best practice in these matters and how applied work should be carried out, but it is difficult to resist the weight of evidence from so many sources that is presented in Friedman and Schwartz's work.

A central concern was the relationship between money and nominal income and the way in which the latter divided between price and output. For Friedman and Schwartz, nominal income is a function of differences between the quantity of money supplied and demanded, and between differences in the growth rates of the quantities of money and output. The underlying assumption is that if a long enough period is taken – and they take a century, which does seem long enough – then the country can be thought of as being on its demand for money function.

The supply of money can therefore be seen as measuring the quantity demanded. Figures 2.1 and 2.2 respectively, show the close correspondence between money and prices in the USA and the UK over the century from 1890 to 1990. What is important is the percentage change in one variable associated with the percentage change in the other. The results could be replicated for as many countries as have reasonably reliable data.

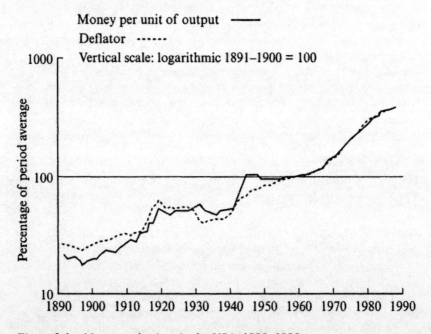

Figure 2.1   Money and prices in the USA, 1890–1990

The figures for the USA and the UK are interesting given the enormous range of experience across the century, and the large differences that were present between the two countries. This was a century that covered different exchange rate regimes (gold standard, floating rates, pegged rates), wars, in the USA the worst depression of all time, and so on. To some extent the strong similarities between the two countries in the period up to 1931 reflect the fact that the gold standard predominated and held the countries together.[5] For the years after 1945, British price performance is much poorer, reflecting the relative lack of discipline in the Bretton Woods system and the failure of Britain to contain monetary growth.

A principal conclusion of Freidman and Schwartz is the following:

> The level of nominal income parallels with great fidelity the level of the nominal quantity of money, and the rate of change of nominal income parallels the rate of change of the nominal quantity of money. That is true for the United States and the United Kingdom and for the whole of the century our data cover. ... This parallelism is a manifestation of the stable demand curve for money plus the excellence of the simple quantity theory approximation. (Friedman & Schwartz, 1982, p. 7)

Similar stories can be told for more recent periods for other countries. For example, Figures 2.3 and 2.4 respectively, show the course of money and prices

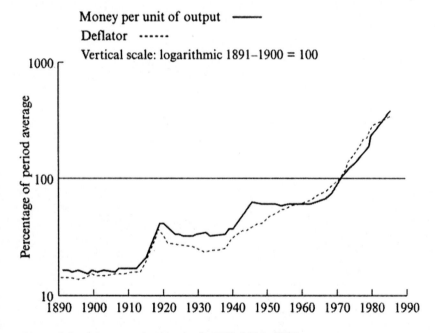

Figure 2.2   Money and prices in the UK, 1890–1990

in Germany and Japan between 1960 and 1990. For both countries the money
stock rose more rapidly than prices. In Germany money grew at 4.8 per cent per
annum, while the consumer price index rose at a rate of 2.7 per cent per annum.
In Japan money grew at 7 per cent and prices at 5.7 per cent per annum. Some
of the difference was reflected in the decline in velocity. The suggestion is that
the very rapid growth in output raised the demand for real money balances. This
was something that had happened in other countries at other times.

This treatment could be extended to a range of other countries where monetary
growth over a long period grew at very rapid rates (as, for example, in Latin
America) and where the corresponding price rises were also very rapid.

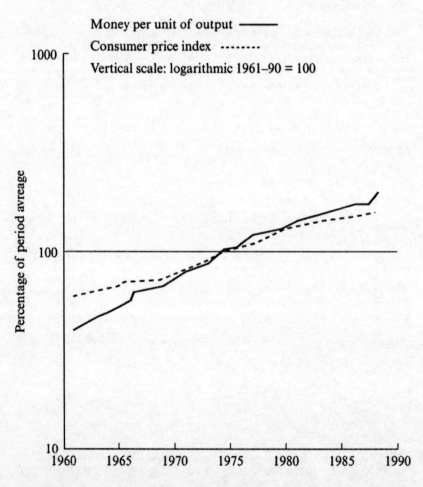

Figure 2.3   Money and prices in Germany, 1960–1990

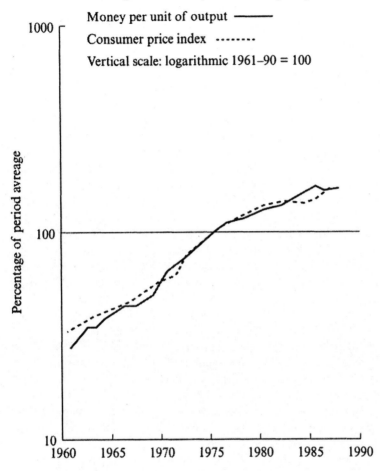

Figure 2.4   *Money and prices in Japan, 1960–1990*

EXTREME EPISODES

At several points in the last two-and-a-half centuries there have been short periods of rather intense experiences when prices have risen at exceedingly rapid rates. It is the argument of this chapter that these experiences provide alternative, supplementary and powerful support for the view that it is the alteration of the money stock that produces changes in prices. The episodes we consider are all those that we know of prior to 1950 where inflation rose to over 100 per cent per annum. They are the American War of Independence in the 1780s, revolutionary France in the 1790s, the USA in the 1860s, and the hyperinflations of the 1920s and the 1940s. (These latter were defined by Cagan as beginning when the rate of inflation rose above 50 per cent per month, and ending when it fell below that rate.)

The following discussion provides the briefest outline, but it can serve to indicate the nature of the processes at work. The first experience was in the American colonies in the second half of the eighteenth century. The rebellion by the colonists (1775–83) could not be financed from taxation since there was no power to tax, not at least by Congress;[6] instead it was done very largely by the issue of paper currency, the 'Continental'. That was supported by some external borrowing and some gifts from foreign powers, but the bulk came from printing money. Prices soared across the eastern colonies, with inflation, for example, reaching over 1000 per cent for the two years 1779–80 in Philadelphia.

In France in the 1790s, following the Revolution, paper money (the assignat), was issued in steadily increasing amounts. Where once paper money had been abhorred, following earlier lessons, it was felt by many that revolutionary France was sufficiently enlightened and sophisticated to be able to use it. By 1795, 45 000 million livres had been issued. A corresponding soaring of prices took place, from a base of 100 in 1790 to 31 000 in September 1795 and 38 850 in May 1796.

Back in the United States, came the next episode of this kind in the civil war of the 1860s. There were differences in the experiences of the North and the South. In the North, taxes and borrowing covered most of the expenditure required to fight the civil war. In the South, the Confederate government, with fewer possibilities for taxing, obtained their supplies by turning to the printing press. Note issue increased by over 82 000 per cent and the money stock rose by 1100 per cent in the space of three years. The worst affected part of the Confederation was in the east, where prices rose from 100 in 1861 to 2300 three years later, and to 9200 by the end of 1865.

In the 1920s there were several cases of hyperinflation. Austria, Hungary, Poland, Russia and Germany all suffered. New governments, unfamiliar with budgetary finance, readily succumbed to the attraction of paper money. Further, in all these cases there were serious doubts over the viability of the state. In Austria and Hungary new arrangements followed the collapse of the Austro-Hungarian empire. Russia was turned upside-down in the Bolshevik Revolution of 1917–20. Poland had similar problems. It saw experienced officials leaving the country and the new state left without proper civil administration. Germany had a new and inexperienced socialist government, and indeed a Bolshevik government in Bavaria. There was widespread social unrest. Parenthetically there were some countries (such as Czechoslovakia) at this time that were similar but which escaped incipient hyperinflation by means of rigorous fiscal programmes.

In the 1940s there were three outstanding cases of hyperinflation: Hungary, Greece and China. Hungary was the worst experience of all time. This is particularly interesting since that country had so recently experienced a hyperinflation and had apparently learned the lesson. However, the second inflation is attributed to the Soviet influence in Hungary after World War II and the desire to wipe out the middle class and speed the dictatorship of the proletariat. China suffered a long and damaging war followed by the fight between the communists and the nationalists. As a result the budget deficit soared, followed closely by monetary expansion and then by rising prices. The Greeks suffered under a despised German occupation and, when that was over, monetary expansion really took off in the struggle between the monarchists and the communists. Again a vast deficit opened up, the printing of money rocketed and prices spiralled – from 100 in 1940 to 163 billion in 1944 and higher still in 1949.

What were the circumstances that produced the dramatic episodes where annual inflation reached heights above 100 per cent, and in many cases far more? It was of course monetary growth that was responsible for the price change. But what lies behind the growth in the money stock? The dominant factor was the need to monetize government deficits, that is to print money to cover the deficit. That is what produced the monetary expansion. The monetization occurred when the growth in government expenditure could not be matched by raising revenue or by borrowing. And what produced this was an imbalance present between those spending and those paying; in other words, when the government was relatively weak in relation to the governed – when it felt unable to impose taxes and took the easier option of printing money. Governments resort to the printing press in order to buy the resources they need to survive.

The first striking feature about all of the episodes listed is that there was a huge expansion of unbacked paper currency and the money stock soared. Such growth was actually impossible without paper money. (Remember that paper currency was rare prior to the twentieth century.) The second striking feature is that in all cases there were large fiscal deficits, which opened up very quickly. When borrowing was limited or impossible, the whole of the deficit had to be monetized.

The question then is, in what circumstance did such budget deficits appear? It is not wartime, as is frequently asserted. There would be many more cases if that were true since the history of the world is essentially one of war. In fact in wartime it is often easier to raise taxes and to borrow (both internally and externally) as an outside foe stimulates patriotism, and the economic costs fade when put alongside the political cost – defeat. Think of Britain in the 100 years from 1690 to 1790. Britain was at war for something like half this period, mostly with France. Taxes rose at a rate far in excess of the rate of growth of income and in addition the national debt soared from £2 million to £230 million at which point it was equal to about 110 per cent of national income.[7] Yet there was no inflation to speak of across that long period. So it is unlikely that it is war that provides the explanation for high inflation.

Instead it turns out to be at times of civil war or serious social unrest, when government spending rises steeply to placate the rebellious element or to fight it, and the tax base shrinks as a result of the division in society. The inflation tax is the one that governments can still use. As Keynes (1923) put it, inflation 'is the form of taxation which the public find hardest to evade and even the weakest government can enforce when it can enforce nothing else'.

In summary, in all these cases of dramatic inflations the explanation is that wild expansion of the money stock was followed by soaring prices. There are plenty of examples of pressures on governments that would have produced inflation, but where they were resisted no monetary expansion took place, and no inflation. Why then do governments resort to overissue of the currency and produce inflation? The evidence from these extreme cases is that it is a last resort in an attempt to save themselves from overthrow. These episodes of very rapid inflation bring out in dramatic fashion how, when governments are under serious pressure, they resort quickly to the printing press and inflation follows equally quickly thereafter.

THE THEORY

The long-run relationship between money and prices is one of the longest established in economics. The theory, too, is amongst the oldest parts of economics. In the eighteenth century the Scottish economist, David Hume (1752) set out the essential elements of the relationship: 'augmentation (in the quantity of money) has no other effect than to heighten the price of labour and commodities ... after prices have settled it has no manner of influence'. And Henry Thornton showed the same awareness when, at the beginning of the nineteenth century, he wrote on how the money supply should be adjusted by the authorities in times of inconvertible currency:

> To limit the amount of paper issued, and to resort for this purpose, whenever the temptation is strong, to some effectual principle of restriction; in no case, however, materially to diminish the sum in circulation, but to let it vibrate only within certain limits; to afford a slow and cautious extension of it, as the general trade of the kingdom enlarges itself; to allow of some special though temporary encrease in the event of any extraordinary alarm or difficulty. (Thornton, 1802, p. 259)

This theoretical basis and practical prescription was, in all its essential elements, widely accepted until the middle of the twentieth century. It is the Friedman rule.[8] Keynes may have sent the train down the wrong track for a while, but it does seem to have come back to the main line now after a long, meandering and wasted tour around the country.

This is not the place to take up the debate on the various strands of thought on the role of money in economic theory. We simply remind the reader of the principal variables and of the relationship that is said to hold amongst them. The variables are those found in the quantity theory: the stock of money, the general price level, the velocity of circulation and the level of output. Our principal focus is on the ratio of the money stock to real output. The theory says that the long-run trend in this ratio will be paralleled by a similar long-run trend in prices – what is called the long-run neutrality of money. In other words, money does not affect any real variables in the long run, and any changes in the money stock not matched by changes in output will be observed in changed prices.

The framework is usually set out in the following way:

$$MV = PT$$

where M is the stock of money, V is the velocity of circulation, P the price level and T the volume of transactions. The velocity of circulation is the number of times the money stock turns over in a given period, and is assumed to be stable. It is stable, but not constant, since there are factors at work that will change velocity; but they work slowly and can be used to predict its path. The quantity of output grows steadily on trend, therefore if money increased rapidly the effect on the right-hand side of the equation would be to raise prices.

However, even if this turns out to be the case, it will still not reveal the direction in which the causality is running. That is to say, does it run from money to prices, or might it be the other way round? We do know that output growth is generally low and stable. Against that, monetary growth can be much more volatile. And it is the excess growth of money in relation to output that is said to produce price rises: 'Inflation occurs when the quantity of money rises appreciably more rapidly than output, and the more rapid the rise in the quantity of money per unit of output, the greater the rate of inflation. There is probably no other proposition in economics that is as well established as this one' (Friedman, 1992, p. 193). It is the fact that output is relatively stable and money growth potentially rapid that makes an examination of the long period in history illuminating.

The argument of this chapter has been that, when the very long run is considered, the above proposition on money and prices is strongly supported. And in addition there is the other evidence from some interesting dramatic episodes. All that evidence seems to point convincingly to the fact that stable money would produce stable prices. Of course there are complications. Once prices start rising they contribute to their own continuing rise via expectations and changing velocity. Further, there can be occasions when income leads money movements, as when, for example, under the gold standard a rise in income raised the demand for money and this in turn (via the balance of payments) attracted money into the economy and so raised the money stock.

But these are likely to be of short duration, and as such not our central concern, and more importantly are unlikely to have price level ramifications.

To revert to the equation $MV = PT$, if M increased suddenly, it would be spent and producers might misread the increase in demand as a rise in demand for their product. That would mean that output would rise, but this would be temporary and the trend path would be returned to after a short period.

CONCLUSION

Over recent decades there has been extensive investigation of the relationship between money and other variables. This has resulted in money being recognized as an extremely important macroeconomic variable. There have been many econometric studies of the long-run relationship between money and prices. Unfortunately, the lack of robust data for very long periods has hampered such studies. And there are also other problems of theoretical and statistical kinds. That is why it is worth turning to an examination of a long sweep of history. The great wealth of material available to us can provide a different perspective on these matters. What an examination of the very long run in history reveals is that there was a clear and close relationship between money and prices over many centuries. But it does more. It serves as a reminder that output growth is generally and moderately stable on trend, and that for most of history money was metallic and its production and circulation rates were also low and stable. The only occasions on which inflation appeared were those when money was somehow expanded, periods of continuous debasement or of inflows of new bullion. The really rapid inflations all came with paper money. The widespread use of the technology that produces paper money only appears in the twentieth century and so too do the worst and most persistent inflations. In other words, we have powerful additional evidence that inflation is always and everywhere a monetary phenomenon.

NOTES

1. I thank Geoffrey Wood for his comments and suggestions on an earlier draft.
2. Thomas Malthus postulated that, while food supply grew in arithmetic progression, population grew in geometrical progression. In the absence of what he called 'moral restraint', the tendency of population to outrun subsistence was held in check by war and famine. Not until the beginnings of modern economic growth did it become possible to escape this Malthusian trap.
3. The usual assumption made in discussion of this is that on trend population is a reasonably good proxy for output.
4. The best estimates of output for this century suggest some gentle expansion.

5. Different experience is expected under different exchange rate regimes. This is most succinctly put by Friedman and Schwartz and is best quoted at length: 'Under a fixed exchange-rate regime, changes in one country affect another through actual or potential discrepancies between the countries in the prices of identical goods and in relative prices of traded and non-traded goods, which in turn alter trade flows and produce species flows and capital movements. Under variable exchange rates, exchange-rate changes replace specie flows wholly or in part, depending on whether the exchange rate floats or is partly controlled by central bank intervention. If exchange rates float freely, the own-country money stocks are insulated from one another, and one channel of influence is closed off. There remain the other two – other country money converted into own-country currency, which will reflect changes in exchange rates as well as in the nominal quantity of money, and velocity. But it would not be surprising if the closing off of one channel affected the operation of the others. (Friedman and Schwartz, 1982, p. 325.)
6. Individual states had some powers to tax.
7. Currently it is somewhere in the region of 50 per cent.
8. Friedman advocated that the money supply should be expanded gradually in line with the long-run growth rate of output.

BIBLIOGRAPHY

Cagan, P. (1969), 'The non-neutrality of money in the long run', *Journal of Money, Credit and Banking*, **1** (2), May, 207–27.

Capie, Forrest (1986), 'Conditions in which very rapid inflation has appeared', *Carnegie–Rochester Conference Series on Public Policy*, **24**.

Capie, Forrest and Ghila Rodrik-Bali, (1983), 'Monetary Growth and Determinants in Britain, 1870–1913', City University, *Monetary History Discussion Paper*, no.-6.

Friedman, Milton (1992), *Money Mischief: episodes in monetary history*, Harcourt, Brace, Jovanovich.

Friedman, Milton and Anna J. Schwartz (1982), *Monetary Trends in the United States and the United Kingdom*, University of Chicago Press.

Hume, David (1752), *Of interest of money*.

Kent, R. (1920), 'The Edict of Diocletian Fixing Maximum Prices', *The University of Pennsylvania Law Review*.

Keynes, J.M. (1923), *A Tract on Monetary Reform*, Macmillan.

Lucas, R. (1980), 'Two illustrations of the quantity theory of money', *American Economic Review*, 1005–15.

Schwartz, Anna J. (1973) 'Secular Price Change in Historical Perspective', *Journal of Money, Credit and Banking*, **70** (11), 243–69.

Thornton, Henry (1802), *Paper Credit*, Augustus Kelley Reprint, 1978.

Wood, G. (1976), 'Wealth, savings and the rate of interest in the long run', *Bulletin of Economic Research*, **28** (2), 104–9.

Wrigley E.A. and R. Schofield (1989), *The Population History of England, 1541–1871*, Cambridge University Press.

3. Why financial stability depends on price stability

Anna J. Schwartz

A mandate to maintain the value of the currency historically was the guiding principle of central banks. That meant that their overriding concern was to maintain the purchasing power of the nation's money. Central banks in this century broadened the objectives they believed themselves capable of attaining. The objectives came to include a high level of employment, economic growth, low interest rates and balance in international payments, in addition to achieving stable prices. However an upsurge of inflation from the mid-1960s to the early 1980s, accompanied by lacklustre real economic gains, bred disillusion with the ambitious list of objectives that central banks had set for themselves. In recent years central banks have shed the broad list and reverted to their historic primary guiding principle – price stability – as their major responsibility.

In explaining their newly proclaimed commitment to price stability, central bankers cite a loss of productivity growth as a result of inflation, and job loss when inflation mounts. Hence concentrating on price stability is a way of fostering improved standards of living and employment. It should be added that financial stability is a further and significant benefit of price stability. Financial stability encompasses the financial condition of the private sector of non-financial firms and households as well as the financial condition of banks and other intermediaries.

Accordingly, it is now widely accepted that price stability should be the goal of monetary policy, and that the economy in many dimensions will benefit if the goal is reached. The contrary is unstated: if inflation and price instability prevail, so also will financial instability.

To understand the relationship between price stability and financial stability, it is useful to begin by reviewing the economic and social features of inflation. Inflation creates uncertainty. The information contained in prices of goods and services is lessened when the aggregate level of prices is changing unpredictably. Moreover the variability of changes in relative prices seems to rise as the overall rate of inflation rises. Business firms, households and government cannot then easily distinguish between relative prices that are advantageous and those that are disadvantageous. It will be hard for them to sort out real price signals from individual price changes that reflect leads and lags in responses to inflationary pressures. They will not make the adjustments to the use of resources in some cases that they should have made, and will adjust the use of resources in other cases where they should not have. Planning for the future also becomes more difficult. How much to save and in what forms become troublesome decisions. For financial intermediaries unpredictable price level changes affect asset prices on their balance sheets and the economic stability of their borrowers.

The social strains that inflation creates are another feature, pitting those who benefit and those who lose in such an environment against one another. Households differ in the type of assets held and the degree to which they are leveraged by debt. Depending on the composition of their assets and on how asset prices behave in inflation, and on their debt burdens, households will be differentially affected.

The usual way of describing the disruptive effects of inflation on financial markets is to report that it leads to a random redistribution of wealth and a dramatic shortening of investment horizons. In unanticipated inflation borrowers repay their debts with devalued currency. In the case of government, the biggest borrower, unanticipated inflation confers an unlegislated increase in taxes. Safety and soundness of financial institutions are imperilled when they make contracts to pay others and receive from others fixed money amounts without knowing whether the price level or the inflation rate they expect will be realized.

To detail the harmful effects of inflation on financial stability, this chapter first offers a microeconomic approach, and then a macroeconomic approach. It continues with a discussion of the costs of inflation, especially in relation to financial instability. The chapter ends with a summary of the argument that the goal of financial stability is attainable by the means of price stability.

A MICROECONOMIC APPROACH TO FINANCIAL EFFECTS OF INFLATION

The microeconomic description of the disruptive effects on financial stability of inflation examines the consequences for the sectoral behaviour of business firms, households, financial intermediaries and government. For business firms, the disruptive effect of inflation here centres on the calculation of profits. For households, the disruptive effect centres on the need for portfolio shifts to alter the composition of balance sheets. For intermediaries, the disruptive effect, due to inflation-induced fluctuations in interest rates, centres on the problem of differences in the maturity structure of their assets and liabilities. Government is the source of inflation and, thanks to increases in its tax receipts, a beneficiary.

At the same time, given nominal accounting methods, government deficits in inflation are overstated.

The microeconomic effects of inflation on each sector follow.

Business Firms

Business profits are misstated in an inflation. To adjust profits measured in current prices, it is necessary to correct for (1) increases in the replacement cost of capital assets and inventory, (2) capital gains on tangible assets, and (3) changes in market value of outstanding debt.

Historical cost accounting reflects allowances for depreciation of capital and cost of materials acquired at earlier prices that no longer prevail for new acquisitions. Capital consumption and inventory valuation must be adjusted to reflect increases in the replacement cost of capital and materials. The correction of capital consumption reduces profits by eliminating understatement of capital consumption that calculating the value of capital at historical cost produces. If companies use the first-in, first-out method of accounting of the cost of materials, they overstate profits and increase income taxes in real terms. Inventory valuation must be based on the last-in, first-out method of accounting to remove the effect of price changes on the cost of material.

A second adjustment of profits in an inflation is necessary if the replacement cost of capital exceeds or falls short of the change in the general price level. The current resource cost of using the capital must either be raised or lowered. The capital gain or loss is the discounted present value of the anticipated change in the stream of real returns to the capital good. The change is reflected in the firm's profits and net worth.

A third adjustment of profits in an inflation is necessary because of changes in the market value of the firm's outstanding financial assets and liabilities due to interest rate changes. The market value of a firm's debt declines when interest rates rise as a result of expectations of higher inflation. That will change the firm's net worth and produce a capital gain.

Inflation distorts the financial record unless accounting corrections are made. The corrections serve to inform firms of their true economic condition in inflation. Inflation imposes this cost on firms to help them avert mistaken decisions in production and resource allocation. Price stability would obviate the need for such accounting corrections.

Households

Households' balance sheet assets are distributed between financial assets (equities, long- and short-term securities, deposits, life insurance, pension funds) and tangible assets (owner-occupied housing, land, consumer durables). In an inflation, households may seek to increase their acquisition of financial liabilities relative to income and avoid financial assets, particularly assets fixed in monetary terms. Financial assets depreciate in real terms, without additional allowance for depreciation from the rise in interest rates. There is an incentive to reduce the share of financial assets and increase the share of tangible assets. This tendency is accentuated when residential property values climb faster than general prices, stimulating acquisition of real property as a hedge against inflation. Yet, because inflation increases uncertainty about the future value of assets, households may desire greater liquidity and hence increase financial saving.

The effect of inflation on household net worth varies, depending on whether households are renters, who are losers, homeowners without mortgages, who are small gainers, or heavily mortgaged homeowners, who are substantial gainers. Clearly, for households as a whole, inflation has been a burden. They would have been better off under stable prices of goods and services.

Financial Intermediaries

Financial institutions and markets must cope with the response of households to inflation. If households shun financial assets, the inflow of funds to financial intermediaries dries up. The main problem intermediaries face in inflation, however, is the impact of high and rising market interest rates on the maturity structure of their balance sheets. Their assets are mostly long term. Since their loans and securities were acquired when interest rates were lower, the average rate of return on their portfolios, once interest rates rise, is below market interest rates. Their liabilities, moreover, are mostly short term. They cannot afford to pay competitive rates on their liabilities and so experience disintermediation.

Had balance sheet losses for such intermediaries been acknowledged, they would have been declared insolvent. This was the situation of many US savings and loan institutions in the 1980s. Some of them sought new loans with the highest possible returns, using brokered deposits to fund the loans. Since the government insured the deposits, the riskiness of the loans was no deterrent to the institutions' managers. Eventually these institutions failed, at enormous cost to US taxpayers.

Some financial intermediaries are not troubled by differences in maturity structure of assets and liabilities. Insurance and pension funds receive contractual contributions from contributors, are obliged to pay out fixed amounts at distant future dates, and in inflation shift their investments to avoid losses. Financial intermediaries in the ordinary course of events seek the best returns on investments, but changes in patterns of asset accumulation, given inflation uncertainty, are a cost of inflation.

Government

Because government revenues rise, owing to the inflation tax, government may increase expenditures. This distorts the interpretation of the economic situation. Under inflation national income is measured incorrectly. As noted, the government deficit in nominal terms is overstated.

Summary

From a microeconomic viewpoint, inflation distorts decisions by business firms and individuals on capital accumulation. It affects valuation of firms on stock markets. It forces changes in patterns of asset accumulation by the private sector in general. Planning ability is diminished. For intermediaries the effect of inflation is unstable financial flows. Book and market valuations of asset prices diverge. Government accounts are distorted, but the government registers nominal gains.

A MACROECONOMIC APPROACH TO FINANCIAL EFFECTS OF INFLATION

Price level stability is essential for financial stability. The increase in bank failure rates worldwide in the 1970s and 1980s occurred in conditions of general price level instability. Banks made loans and investments that appeared sound when inflation prevailed. Disinflation that followed undermined credit evaluations on which the banks based their decisions. Price level stability accordingly promotes sound banking.

In the postwar decades until the mid-1960s, banking systems in the major industrialized countries were generally free of problem institutions. The question is why financial systems since then have been plagued by insolvencies. The answer is that the world price level was relatively stable in the earlier period, but subsequently was marked first by inflationary surges and then by disinflationary plunges. It was price level gyrations that contributed to financial instability.

The reason that price instability confounds financial stability is related to the way financial institutions conduct credit analysis. As a condition for a secured loan, a lender will require collateral, the value of which must be assessed. As a condition for an unsecured loan of working capital, a lender will project the ratio of a borrower's current assets to his current liabilities. The lender bases both the estimate of a would-be borrower's balance sheet ratios and the valuation of collateral on his presumption of the continuation for the life of the loan of the current price level or inflation rate. Unexpected changes in the price level or inflation rate can invalidate the assumptions on which the loan was based.

The management of a financial institution's bond portfolio is also conditioned by beliefs concerning the future price level and interest rates. Holding periods of bonds, it is true, can be altered more readily than commercial and industrial loans when underlying conditions that justified the extension of credit change unpredictably, but the fact remains that price instability undermines sound banking. It contributes to financial risk. Moreover price variability is a breeding ground for fraud and mismanagement of financial institutions.

There is a recent literature in the USA on asymmetric information that focuses on the differences in information available to the two parties in a financial contract (Mishkin, 1991). According to this approach borrowers have better information than lenders about the prospects of investment projects the former want to undertake. The asymmetric information approach is combined with the approach proposed in the 'lemons' problem literature (Akerlof, 1970). The argument offered is that adverse selection occurs in the loan market, and this explains disruption in financial markets that affects aggregate economic activity adversely.

In brief, financial markets in the foregoing literature are characterized by lenders who cannot distinguish between borrowers of good quality and those of bad quality (the 'lemons'). Hence lenders charge an interest rate that averages the quality of good and bad borrowers, so high-quality borrowers pay a higher rate than they should and low-quality borrowers a lower rate than they should. As a result borrowers with the riskiest projects are the likeliest to take out loans. Uncertainty increases because lenders cannot discriminate between good and bad borrowers, and the adverse selection problem worsens.

This literature appears to mischaracterize financial markets. Asymmetric information is not the problem confronting lenders and borrowers. Both evaluate the prospects of projects borrowers want to undertake by extrapolating the prevailing price level or inflation rate. Borrowers default on loans, not because they have misled uninformed lenders, but because, subsequent to the initiation of the project, authorities have altered monetary policy in a contractionary direction. The original price level and inflation rate assumptions are no longer valid. The change in monetary policy makes rate of return calculations on the yield of projects, based on the initial price assumptions of both lenders and borrowers, unrealizable. Borrowers lose the sums they have invested. Lenders have to contend with losses on loans.

It is this sequence of events that illustrates why monetary stability that establishes price stability matters for financial stability. If central banks are now truly committed to achieving and preserving price stability, the dividends of this commitment will be not only higher productivity growth, improved standards of living and rising employment, as they have contended, but, most certainly, greater financial stability.

COSTS OF INFLATION

Economists at one time limited the measurement of the cost of inflation to the effect of a predictable tax on money balances. The cost of inflation on this view was trivial. To economize on the cost of holding non-interest-bearing money balances because of the negative real rate on money during inflation involved at most a modest amount. The cost was derisively named the shoe-leather cost – more trips to the bank. That cost has been estimated to amount only to 0.03 per cent of GDP, assuming low inflation rates (Fischer, 1994).

As the inflation rate rises, however, the cost of minimizing money balances also rises. Business firms and households reallocate their efforts from production and distribution of goods to stratagems of delaying payments and urgent switching of cash receipts into very short-term income-earning assets. The cost of these actions has been estimated as approximated by the square of the inflation rate.

Additional generally unquantified costs of inflation, anticipated and unanticipated, include costs of frequent price changes for firms, distortions due to nominal accounting results of nominal contract obligations, effects on investment decisions, changes in patterns of asset accumulation and misallocation of resources among sectors. Taken together, the cost of these distortions has been estimated at 2–5 per cent of GDP at an inflation rate of 10 per cent.

The cost estimates, as tenuous as they are, overlook what may be regarded as the real costs of financial instability in a regime of unstable prices. One would need to tot up the losses on all the construction projects, factories and transport systems that are abandoned when the price assumptions under which they were begun prove to be illusory. In addition, one would need to account for the projects that were not undertaken because of reluctance to make future commitments without knowledge of prices. Gross losses on the former set of projects may be reduced when they are bought after bankruptcy and brought to completion by new investors, but net losses remain.

This view does not imply that project failures occur only because of price instability that makes untenable advance calculation of their prospects. In a market economy random business failures also occur during periods of price stability. They occur then because of faulty judgments about demand and market size, because of low-quality product and mismanagement of enterprises, because bankers' loan standards are sometimes lax. These are failures predominantly of going concerns. What is striking, however, is that the losses that creditors suffered because of non-financial firm failures during stable prices, for example, from the 1950s to the mid-1960s, did not precipitate financial firm failures.

Price instability failures tend to cluster in projects brought to a halt before completion, in sectors most vulnerable to changes in monetary policy, such as construction. This record of losses as a result of price instability does not exhaust the cost consequences. In addition, the record must also include the adverse outcomes for financial intermediaries, ranging from insolvency to declines in stock market valuation and profitability.

Estimates of the cost of inflation that minimize its effects on GDP omit consideration of the losses firms and financial intermediaries suffer when monetary policy is reversed to bring inflation down. The costs can be avoided by a regime of monetary and price stability.

CONCLUSIONS

In industrialized economies accounts are kept in nominal money amounts. With stable prices the accounts reveal the true economic condition of firms and households. No adjustments are needed for discrepancies between historical and current costs. Inflation-induced fluctuations in interest rates are obviated. Asset accumulation can be guided by holders' tastes for risk and relative asset prices without consideration of unpredictable changes in aggregate prices. Financial institutions experience stable financial flows and are not compelled to alter the maturity structure of their balance sheets or the patterns of their asset accumulations in the absence of unstable prices. Microeconomic financial stability is achievable with stable prices.

The perceptions of lenders and borrowers in evaluating projects are not distorted when they can count on the persistence of the price level (or inflation rate) that prevails at their initiation. When the original price level or inflation rate assumptions are invalidated by unpredictable monetary policy changes, not only do projects fail, but borrowers go bankrupt, and financial intermediaries bear capital losses and the risk of failure. Monetary stability is a prerequisite of price stability, and price stability is a prerequisite of financial stability.

A regime of monetary and price stability is the route to financial stability. Such a regime avoids the quantifiable and unquantifiable costs of price instability in distorting economic performance.

REFERENCES

Akerlof, George A. (1970), 'The Market for Lemons: Qualitative Uncertainty and the Market Mechanism', *Quarterly Journal of Economics*, **84** (August), 488–500.
Fischer, Stanley (1994), 'Modern Central Banking', *The Future of Central Banking: The Tercentenary Symposium of the Bank of England*, Cambridge: Cambridge University Press, 202–308.
Mishkin, Frederic S. (1991), '*Asymmetric Information and Financial Crises: A Historical Perspective*', in R. G. Hubbard (ed.), *Financial Markets and Financial Crises*, Chicago: University of Chicago Press, pp. 69–108.

4. Monetary regimes and economic performance: lessons from history

Michael D. Bordo

INTRODUCTION

Which monetary regime is best for economic performance? One based on convertibility into specie (gold and or silver), in which the monetary authority defines its monetary unit in terms of a fixed weight of specie and ensures that paper money claims on the specie monetary unit are always interchangeable for specie? Or one based on government fiat? Alternatively, in the international monetary sphere, which international monetary regime is superior? One based on fixed exchange rates? One based on floating rates? Or some intermediate variant such as the adjustable peg that characterized the Bretton Woods system and the European Monetary System (EMS)? Or the managed float which prevails in the world today?

Before attempting to answer these questions we define a monetary regime as a set of monetary arrangements and institutions accompanied by a set of expectations – expectations by the public with respect to policy makers' actions and expectations by policy makers about the public's reaction to their actions. Thus, for example, under a convertible regime, expectations about the long-run pattern of the price level tend to be mean reverting, that is, the public expects that periods of rising prices will be offset by periods of declining prices. By contrast, under a discretionary fiat money regime, inflation expectations would be extrapolative (Leijonhufvud, 1984), that is, the public would expect that a rising inflation rate would continue indefinitely into the future.

Two types of regimes have prevailed in history: those based on convertibility into specie and those based on fiat. The former prevailed in various guises until Richard Nixon closed the gold window in August 1971, thereby terminating the gold convertibility feature of the Bretton Woods international monetary system. The latter is the norm worldwide today. Regimes have both a domestic and an international aspect. The domestic aspect pertains to the monetary arrangements which determine the domestic money supply. The international aspect relates to the monetary arrangements between countries. Two basic types of international monetary arrangements prevail – fixed and flexible exchange rates – along with a number of intermediate variants including adjustable pegs and managed floating. In the case of convertible regimes, if a number of countries defined their currencies in terms of the same precious metal, gold, for instance, they would adhere to a fixed exchange rate. If countries defined their countries in terms of different metals, some to gold and some to silver, for example, their exchange rates would float. Similarly, under a fiat money regime, nations could follow either fixed or floating rates, depending on mutually agreed upon arrangements.

A key question is which regime gives the best economic performance. Traditional theory posits that a convertible regime, such as the classical gold standard which prevailed from 1880 to 1914, is characterized by a set of self-regulating market forces that tend to ensure long-run price level stability. These forces operate through the classical commodity theory of money (Bordo, 1984). According to that theory, substitution between monetary and non monetary uses of gold and changes in production will eventually offset any inflationary or deflationary price level movements. The problem is that unexpected shocks to the supply or demand for gold can have significant short-run effects on the price level. In an international convertible regime, pegging nations' currencies to the fixed price of gold provides a stable nominal anchor to the international monetary system. Such stability, however, comes at the expense of exposure to foreign shocks through the balance of payments which in the presence of wage and price stickiness can produce volatile output and employment. Adherence to the international convertible regime also implies a loss of monetary independence since under such a regime the monetary authorities' prime commitment is to maintain convertibility of their currencies into the precious metal and not to stabilize the domestic economy.

In a fiat money regime, in theory, monetary authorities could use open market operations, or other policy tools, to avoid the types of shocks that may jar the price level under a specie standard and hence provide both short-run and long-run price stability. In addition to giving monetary authorities the independence to pursue stable prices, adhering to a flexible exchange rate fiat regime provides insulation against foreign shocks.[1]

As in a convertible regime, countries following fiat money regimes can adhere to fixed exchange rates with each other. The key advantage of doing so is to avoid the transactions cost of exchange. However a fixed rate system based on fiat money may not provide the stable nominal anchor of the specie convertibility regime unless all the members define their currencies in terms of the currency of one dominant country (such as the USA under Bretton Woods or Germany in the EMS), which country in turn follows a rule which requires it to maintain price stability. Alternatively the members collectively formulate a mechanism to ensure world price stability such as to create an international central bank constrained to maintain it. Finally, in a fiat money flexible rate regime, the absence of the nominal anchor of the fixed price of specie opens up the possibility that monetary authorities, to satisfy the government's fiscal demands, or to maintain full employment, could use the printing press to engineer high inflation.

The theoretical literature concludes that it is difficult to provide an unambiguous ranking of exchange rate arrangements. Hence empirical evidence on the performance of alternative monetary regimes is crucial in assessing which regime is best for welfare.[2]

Table 4.1 contains annual data on two key measures of economic performance: the (GNP deflator) inflation rate and real per capita GNP for the G-7 industrialized countries. Performance is based on four regimes: the classical gold standard (1881–1913); the inter-war period (1919–39); Bretton Woods (1946–70); and the present floating exchange rate regime (1971–89).[3] The Bretton Woods period is divided into two subperiods: the preconvertible phase (1946–58) and the convertible phase (1959–70).[4] For each variable and each country two summary statistics are presented: the mean and standard deviation. As a summary statistic for the countries taken as a group, the table shows the grand mean.[5] Comments follow on the statistical results for each variable.

Inflation

Countries using the classical gold standard had the lowest rate of inflation and displayed mild deflation during the inter-war period. The rate of inflation during the Bretton Woods period was on average and for every country except Japan lower than during the subsequent floating exchange rate period. The average rate of inflation in the two Bretton Woods subperiods was virtually the same.[6]

The Bretton Woods convertible subperiod had the most stable inflation rate of any regime as judged by the standard deviation. By contrast, the preconvertible Bretton Woods period exhibited greater inflation variability than either the gold standard period or the recent floating exchange rate period.

The evidence of lower inflation and lower inflation variability under the gold standard and Bretton Woods regimes than under the recent float is consistent with the view that convertible regimes provide a stable nominal anchor. The behaviour of two other nominal variables buttresses this conclusion (Bordo 1993a). First, money growth was generally lowest and most stable under the gold standard across all countries, followed by the Bretton Woods convertible regime. Second, long-term nominal interest rates were lowest during the classical gold standard period, and during Bretton Woods they were lower than in the recent float. They were most stable in both convertible regimes. Further evidence for the importance of the convertible regime nominal anchor derives from studies which show that inflation persistence – the extent to which

Table 4.1 Descriptive statistics of inflation and real per capita growth in G-7 countries, 1881–1989 annual data (mean, standard deviation)

	Gold standard (1881–1913)		Inter-war (1919–1938)		Bretton Woods (total) (1946–1970)		Bretton Woods (preconvertible) (1946–1958)		Bretton Woods (convertible) (1958–1970)		Floating exchange (1974–1989)	
	Mean	SD	Mean	SD	Mean	SD	Mean	SD	Mean	SD	Mean	SD
Inflation PGNP*												
United States	0.3	3.1	−1.8	7.6	2.4	2.6	2.8	3.5	2.6	1.5	5.6	2.4
United Kingdom	0.3	3.1	−1.5	7.8	3.7	2.2	4.6	2.5	3.4	1.5	9.4	6.1
Germany	0.6	2.6	−2.1	4.7	2.7	4.0	2.1	6.2	3.2	1.8	3.3	1.2
France	0.0	4.9	2.2	9.1	5.6	4.1	5.6	5.1	5.5	3.6	8.8	3.2
Japan	4.6	5.5	−1.7	7.3	4.5	4.6	4.7	7.3	5.1	1.3	2.6	2.4
Canada	0.4	1.4	−1.9	6.1	2.7	3.0	3.9	3.9	2.9	1.5	7.3	2.6
Italy	0.6	3.2	−1.1	11.7	3.8	11.5	5.8	16.0	3.8	2.1	12.9	4.6
Grand mean	1.0	3.4	−1.1	7.8	3.6	4.6	4.2	6.4	3.9	1.9	7.1	3.2
Real per capita growth*												
United States	1.8	5.1	0.0	8.1	2.0	2.8	1.8	3.4	2.9	1.9	2.1	2.7
United Kingdom	1.1	2.4	1.2	4.5	2.1	1.8	2.1	2.2	2.3	1.4	1.5	4.2
Germany	1.7	2.9	2.6	8.5	5.0	3.3	7.3	3.9	3.5	2.6	2.1	1.9
France	1.5	4.6	1.3	7.2	3.9	2.1	4.6	2.7	3.9	1.3	1.7	1.5
Japan	1.4	3.8	2.0	6.1	8.1	2.7	5.7	1.1	8.9	2.5	3.5	1.1
Canada	2.3	2.8	0.2	8.8	2.5	2.6	2.4	3.3	3.5	1.7	1.3	2.4
Italy	1.0	4.0	0.9	4.7	5.6	3.3	5.2	4.4	5.8	1.9	2.5	2.2
Grand mean	1.5	3.7	1.2	6.8	4.2	2.7	4.2	3.0	4.4	1.9	2.1	2.3

Sources: See Appendix to Bordo (1993a).
Note: * Mean growth rate calculated as the time coefficient from a regression of the natural logarithm of the variable on a constant and a time trend.

45

the rate of inflation is correlated between successive years – for each of the countries in Table 4.1 was lowest during the classical gold standard, followed by the inter-war period, Bretton Woods and the float.[7]

Real Per-capita Income Growth

Generally, the Bretton Woods period, especially the convertible period, exhibited the most rapid output growth of any monetary regime and, not surprisingly, the inter-war period the lowest. Output variability was also lowest in the convertible subperiod of Bretton Woods but, because of higher variability in the preconvertibility period, the Bretton Woods system as a whole was more variable than the floating exchange rate period. Both pre-World War II regimes exhibit higher variability than their post World War II counterpart, with the classical gold standard for the G-7 aggregate almost twice as variable.[8]

In sum, the descriptive evidence in Table 4.1 links convertible regimes with superior nominal performance consistent with the traditional theory, but it is mixed with respect to real performance. The Bretton Woods convertible period exhibited the most rapid and most stable growth of any period, but the classical gold standard, though exhibiting respectable growth, was considerably less stable than any of the postwar regimes.

An important issue is the extent to which the performance of alternative monetary regimes as revealed by the data in Table 4.1 reflects the operation of the monetary regime in constraining policy actions or the presence or absence of shocks to the underlying environment. One way to shed light on this issue is to identify underlying shocks to aggregate supply and demand.[9] Aggregate supply shocks reflect shocks to the environment and are independent of the regime, but aggregate demand shocks likely reflect policy actions and are specific to the regime.

Table 4.2 presents the standard deviations of supply (permanent) and demand (temporary) shocks for the G-7 countries and an aggregate of them for each of the regimes demarcated in Table 4.1. The shocks were calculated from a two-variable vector autoregression in the rate of change of the price level and real output.[10]

Table 4.2 shows for the G-7 aggregate that the convertible Bretton Woods regime was the most tranquil of all the regimes: neither supply nor demand shocks dominated. However it was not that much less turbulent than the succeeding float. The inter-war period, unsurprisingly, shows the largest supply and demand shocks. Sizeable supply and demand shocks which are two or three times greater than the post-World War II period also characterize the classical gold standard.

For individual countries, the Bretton Woods convertible period was the most stable in four countries and flexible rates in three. However, the difference

Table 4.2 *Supply (permanent) and demand (temporary) shocks, 1880–1989 annual data (standard deviations of shocks, per cent)*

	Gold standard 1883–1913		Inter-war 1921–1939		Bretton Woods (total) 1948–1970		Bretton Woods (preconvertible) 1948–1958		Bretton Woods (convertible) 1959–1970		Floating exchange 1973–1989		Post-WWII 1948–1989	
	D	S	D	S	D	S	D	S	D	S	D	S	D	Ss
USA	2.03	3.81	4.45	6.73	2.33	1.54	3.11	1.98	1.37	1.07	1.72	1.94	2.07	1.68
UK	2.66	2.16	1.93	3.52	2.62	1.95	3.06	2.61	2.26	1.14	3.57	4.31	3.03	3.10
Germany	2.37	2.32	4.47	3.13	2.88	2.65	1.85	2.87	3.34	2.66	1.66	1.39	2.36	2.20
France	4.58	3.75	7.17	5.19	3.50	1.75	3.23	1.61	3.77	1.84	1.93	1.52	2.84	1.70
Japan	4.85	3.39	6.28	5.36	3.18	2.56	4.05	1.97	2.83	2.78	2.39	2.50	2.75	2.69
Canada	0.93	2.75	4.01	8.61	2.42	2.60	3.09	3.70	1.74	0.98	2.66	2.10	2.48	2.47
Italy	3.16	3.13	7.40	4.14	2.76	1.75	2.93	1.85	2.56	1.73	3.58	1.91	3.30	2.47
G-7 aggregate data	1.56	2.21	3.09	4.12	1.24	0.86	1.99	1.00	0.75	0.80	1.50	0.96	1.40	0.91

Source: Table 4, Bordo (1993a).

47

between the convertible Bretton Woods period and the float was not great in any country. The inter-war period, as expected, was the most volatile with both types of shocks being the largest in every country except the UK. Finally, in the majority of countries, with the principal exceptions of the UK and Germany, both supply and demand shocks were considerably greater in the gold standard period than in the post-World War II period.[11]

In sum, the evidence on supply and demand shocks suggests that the superior real performance of the Bretton Woods convertible period may have a lot to do with the lower incidence of supply and demand shocks compared to the gold standard and inter-war periods. Greater stability of real output under the Bretton Woods convertible regime may also be explained by adherence to the convertibility rules of the Bretton Woods system by the USA and other industrialized countries. According to Eichengreen (1993) the credibility of commitment to the nominal anchor, as evidenced by the low degree of inflation persistence under Bretton Woods, made inflationary expectations mean reverting. This produced a flatter short-run aggregate supply curve than under the float, where, in the absence of a nominal anchor, inflationary expectations became extrapolative. Under these conditions, stabilization policy could be effective in stabilizing output, that is, in offsetting supply shocks.[12]

That activist stabilization policy is in the main responsible for the low real output variability under Bretton Woods is, however, doubtful. For the USA, activist Keynesian policies were more a product of the late 1960s and 1970s and, for the other countries, a conflict between internal and external balance dominated policy making. A more likely explanation for real output stability is the absence of serious supply shocks.

The evidence from Table 4.2 raises the interesting question as to why the classical gold standard was so durable in the face of substantial shocks (it lasted approximately 35 years), whereas Bretton Woods was so fragile (the convertible phase lasted only 12 years) in the face of the mildest shocks in the past century. One possible answer is more rapid adjustment of prices and output to shocks under the gold standard than under the postwar regimes. Evidence in Bordo (1993a) and Bayoumi and Eichengreen (1994), based on calculations from the impulse response functions derived from the bivariate autoregressions underlying Table 4.2, reveals that the response of output to both demand and supply shocks for the G-7 aggregate and for most of the individual countries was markedly more rapid under the gold standard than under the postwar regimes – and within the postwar regimes was slightly more rapid under the Bretton Woods than the float. The response of prices to both demand and supply shocks was considerably more rapid during the gold standard (and the inter-war period) than under the postwar regimes for the G-7 and most countries. Within the postwar period, it was considerably more rapid under Bretton Woods than under the floating period.

Perhaps the gold standard was able to endure the greater shocks that it faced owing to both greater price flexibility and greater factor mobility before World War I. Alternatively, the gold standard was more durable than Bretton Woods because before World War I the suffrage was limited, central banks were often privately owned and, before Keynes, there was less understanding of the link between monetary policy and the level of economic activity. Hence there was less of an incentive for the monetary authorities to pursue full employment policies which would threaten adherence to convertibility.

REGIME PERFORMANCES AND CREDIBLE COMMITMENT MECHANISMS

An alternative explanation for the relative longevity of the international gold standard and the short life of Bretton Woods may be the design of the monetary regime and specifically the presence or absence of a credible commitment mechanism (or a monetary rule). Both the classical gold standard and the Bretton Woods systems can be viewed as following a series of rules based on the convertibility of domestic currency into gold. Under the classical gold standard the monetary authorities committed themselves to fixing the prices of their currencies in terms of a fixed weight of gold and to buy and sell gold freely in unlimited amounts. The pegged gold price served as a commitment mechanism to prevent monetary authorities from pursuing otherwise time-inconsistent policies (Bordo and Kydland, 1995).

The absence of such a credible commitment mechanism leads governments, in pursuing stabilization policies, to produce an inflationary outcome (Kydland and Prescott, 1977; Barro and Gordon, 1983). In a closed economy environment, once the monetary authority has announced a given rate of monetary growth, which the public expects it to validate, the authority has an incentive to create a monetary surprise – to follow a time-inconsistent policy – either to reduce unemployment or to capture seigniorage revenue. The public, with rational expectations, will come to anticipate the authorities' perfidy, leading to an inflationary equilibrium. A credible commitment mechanism, by preventing the government from cheating, can preserve long-run price stability.

A second relevant example is in the use of fiscal policy. Governments use debt finance to smooth tax revenues over time. When faced with unusual government expenditures, such as in wartime, it is more efficient to sell bonds than to impose higher taxes which can reduce work effort at the time of greatest need. The debt is issued on the assumption that taxes will be raised once the emergency is past in order to service and reduce the debt. In this context, a time-inconsistent fiscal policy would be to impose a capital levy or to default on the debt, once the public has purchased it. Following such a policy would capture additional resources for the government in the present, but in the event of a future emergency would make it very difficult for the government to sell its bonds at favourable prices. A credible commitment mechanism such as the pledge to fix the price of a country's currency in terms of gold can force the government to honour its outstanding debt.

The gold standard rule followed in the century before World War I can be viewed as a form of contingent rule or rule with escape clauses (Bordo and Kydland, 1996). The monetary authority would maintain the standard – keep the price of the currency in terms of specie fixed – except in the event of a well understood emergency such as a major war. In wartime it may suspend gold convertibility and issue paper money to finance its expenditures, and it can sell debt issues in terms of the nominal value of its currency, on the understanding that debt will eventually be paid off in specie. The rule is contingent in the sense that the public understands that the suspension will only last for the duration of the wartime emergency plus some period of adjustment. It assumes that afterwards the government will follow the deflationary policies necessary to resume payments at the original parity. It is important that the rule be transparent and simple and that only a limited number of contingencies be included. Transparency and simplicity would avoid problems of moral hazard and incomplete information, that is, it would make it easier for the public to verify whether the authorities are following the rule.

The gold standard rule originally evolved as a domestic rule enforced by reputation and constitutional guarantees but, because most countries by 1880 adhered to the fixed gold price, it became an international rule. For the international system, the key rule was maintenance of gold convertibility at the established par. The international rule was likely enforced by England, the centre of the gold standard through use of the Bank of England's discount rate policy (Bordo, 1981; Giovannini, 1989), buttressed by cooperation by the central banks of the other core countries, France and Germany (Eichengreen, 1992) and by access for peripheral countries to the capital markets of the core countries.

The classical gold standard regime was successful until it was suspended at the outbreak of World War I. It worked because the credible commitment by the monetary authorities of the core countries to maintain convertibility above all else allowed the contingency clause to accommodate major shocks, and because central bank cooperation eased market pressure in the face of speculative attacks. By contrast, for peripheral countries, the credibility of commitment to the gold standard was considerably weaker, reflecting strong domestic political pressures to alter exchange rates (Bordo and Schwartz, 1996).

The inter-war gold exchange standard which prevailed for only six years was an attempt to recreate the classical gold standard with lower gold reserves and greater freedom for domestic financial policy. As an application of the contingent rule it was much less successful. Because monetary policy was highly politicized in many countries, the commitment to credibility was not believed and devaluation would have led to destabilizing capital flows. Unlike what happened under the prewar gold standard, central bank cooperation was ineffective (Eichengreen, 1992). The system collapsed between 1931 and 1936 in the face of the shocks of the Great Depression.

Bretton Woods was the world's last convertible regime. It can be viewed within the context of the gold standard rule, although it is a distant variant of the original gold standard. The architects of the Bretton Woods conference in 1944, John Maynard Keynes for the UK and Harry Dexter White for the USA, wanting to combine the flexibility and freedom for policy makers of a floating rate system with the nominal stability of the gold standard rule, created an adjustable peg exchange rate system. Under the rules of Bretton Woods, only the USA, as central reserve country and provider of the nominal anchor, was required to peg its currency to gold; the other members were required to peg their currencies to the dollar (Bordo, 1993b).

They were also encouraged to use domestic stabilization policy to offset temporary disturbances. The Bretton Woods system had an escape clause for its members – a change in parity (the adjustable peg) was allowed in the face of a fundamental disequilibrium, which could encompass the contingencies under the gold standard rule – but it was not the same as under the gold standard because it did not require restoring the original parity. Capital controls were encouraged to give members a degree of policy autonomy. The rule for members (other than the USA) was enforced, as under the gold standard, by access to US capital and to the IMF's resources. For the United States, the centre country, the rule was to fix the gold price of the dollar at $35.00 per ounce and to maintain price stability. However, if a majority of members (and every member with 10 per cent or more of the total quotas) agreed, the USA could change the dollar price of gold. There was no explicit enforcement mechanism other than reputation and the commitment to gold convertibility.

As is well known, the system got off to a bad start with Britain's unsuccessful attempt to restore dollar convertibility in 1947 and then her devaluation in September 1949, followed by a large number of countries. The speculative attacks accompanying that event seemed to discourage members from using the escape clause of devaluation in the event of fundamental disequilibrium and encouraged them to utilize capital controls and other means to preserve their parities longer than was consistent with fundamentals. In addition, the contingencies under which changes in parities could occur were not as clear-cut as under the classical gold standard. Fundamental disequilibrium was originally intended to mean the types of shocks that occurred beyond the control of the domestic monetary and fiscal activities. As events unfolded key countries, such as France in 1957, 1958 and 1969 and Britain in 1967, may have devalued as a consequence of lax financial policies. As capital controls became less effective and the markets understood that governments were following policies inconsistent with exchange rate stability, speculative attacks became more serious.

Ultimately the system was successful as long as the USA, the nominal anchor to the system, maintained its commitment to convertibility; that is, maintained price stability. As events turned out, by following highly expansionary monetary and fiscal policies to finance the Vietnam War beginning in the mid-1960s, the USA attached greater importance to domestic concerns than to its role as the centre of the international monetary system, thus weakening it until its collapse in 1971. Thus, although the Bretton Woods system can be interpreted as one based on rules, the system did not provide a credible commitment mechanism. The USA was unwilling to subordinate domestic considerations to the responsibility of maintaining a nominal anchor. At the same time, other major industrialized countries became increasingly unwilling to follow the dictates of the US imposed world inflation rate.

Like the gold standard, Bretton Woods was a convertible regime. Like the gold standard, it was associated with a high degree of macroeconomic stability compared to the inter-war period and the subsequent floating exchange rate regime. Like the gold standard, Bretton Woods was based on a contingent rule. But the Bretton Woods system was less durable than the gold standard. This may reflect the fact that the rules were not well designed: the contingency under which the escape clause mechanism would be invoked was not made clear. It may reflect the lack of a credible commitment by the USA to maintaining price stability. Finally, as argued by an earlier generation of scholars, it may reflect the inherent design flaw of a gold exchange standard – which is what Bretton Woods evolved into – that, as dollar reserves of the rest of the world increase relative to the monetary gold holdings of the centre country, the likelihood of a run on the monetary gold stock of the reserve centre increases.

In light of the Bretton Woods failure, the question arises whether one could devise a better system devoid of its defects. The EMS can be viewed as just such an attempt to establish an adjustable peg regime for a limited number of countries. Like Bretton Woods, it was based on a set of fixed parities called the Exchange Rate Mechanism. Intervention and adjustment were to be financed under a complicated set of arrangements, designed to overcome the weaknesses of the IMF during Bretton Woods. Finally, like Bretton Woods, members could (and did) impose capital controls that were recently phased out. After a shaky start, from 1979 to 1985, the EMS was successful at stabilizing both nominal and real exchange rates within Europe and at reducing divergences between members' inflation rates. The success of the EMS was attributed in large measure to its evolution as an asymmetrical system, like Bretton Woods, with Germany strongly committed to low inflation, acting as the centre country.

Despite its favourable performance for a number of years, the EMS was subjected in 1992 to the same kinds of stress that plagued Bretton Woods. Though the fundamental cause of the crisis was similar in the two regimes, the source of the problem differed. Under Bretton Woods, the shock that led to its collapse was an acceleration of inflation in the USA. Under the EMS, the shock was bond-financed German reunification and the Bundesbank's subsequent deflationary policy. In each case, the system broke down because other countries were unwilling to go along with the policies of the centre country. The commitments to price stability by both the centre country and the other members were revealed to be not credible. Under Bretton Woods, Germany and other Western European countries were reluctant to inflate or to revalue, the USA reluctant to devalue. Under the EMS, the UK, Italy, Spain and Ireland were unwilling to deflate and Germany was unwilling to revalue. As under Bretton Woods, although the EMS has the option for a general realignment, both improved capital mobility and the Maastrich commitment to a unified currency made it an unrealizable outcome.

Thus the lesson from Bretton Woods and the EMS is that pegged exchange rate systems do not work for long, no matter how well they are designed. Pegged exchange rates, capital mobility and policy autonomy just do not mix. The case made years ago, during the Bretton Woods era, for floating exchange rates for major countries still holds. True, European countries could form a currency union with perfectly fixed exchange rates if member countries were wholeheartedly willing to give up domestic policy autonomy but the likelihood that the USA, Japan and even Germany would be willing to accept the loss of sovereignty entailed by moving back to a system like Bretton Woods, as has been recently advocated,[13] seems remote.

The advent of general floating in 1973 and its longevity suggests that the lessons of Bretton Woods have been well learned. Countries are not willing to subject their domestic policy autonomy to that of another country whose commitment they cannot be sure of in a stochastic world or to a supernational monetary authority they cannot control. The key advantage of floating stressed a generation ago by Milton Friedman and Harry Johnson – the freedom to pursue an independent monetary policy – still holds today. In the absence of the credible nominal anchor provided by adherence to gold convertibility, major countries can design credible monetary policy rules to achieve domestic price stability without the costs of giving up their policy autonomy. Proposals such as Friedman's (1960) constant money growth rule, and the McCallum (1988), Meltzer (1987) and Feldstein and Stock (1994) proposals for a monetary base rule with feedback, could provide a credible commitment mechanism to ensure a greater degree of price stability than under the variants of the gold standard. Alternatively the institutional arrangements recently adopted by several countries to create an independent central bank whose sole responsibility is to preserve price stability may also provide the requisite foundations for a credible commitment to price stability.

CONCLUSION

Our survey of evidence on the historical performance of monetary regimes reveals that adherence to the rule of gold convertibility provided a successful stable nominal anchor for both the gold standard and the convertible Bretton Woods regime. The evidence for real performance is less clear-cut across regimes: while the Bretton Woods convertible period was the most stable, the gold standard clearly was not. The diverse real performance can in part be explained by a higher incidence of supply shocks in the pre-World War II period. It is doubtful that the Bretton Woods convertible period's good record is largely due to judicious policy making.

Though associated with superior economic performance, the Bretton Woods convertible regime was very short-lived, lasting a third as long as the classical gold standard and half as long as the succeeding managed float which still exists. The durability of the classical gold standard and tranquillity of Bretton Woods we attribute to regime design. The classical gold standard was so durable because it was based on a credible commitment by the core countries to the contingent gold standard rule. The Bretton Woods adjustable peg exchange rate system can also be viewed as a distant variant of the gold standard rule, but it was short-lived because of design flaws with the adjustable peg and ultimately because of the absence of a credible commitment mechanism by the dominant member, the USA. The EMS, designed to overcome the design flaws of Bretton Woods, collapsed in 1992 under circumstances similar to the demise of Bretton Woods. The lesson from both experiences is that major countries today are basically unwilling to subordinate their monetary sovereignty to the dictates of either an adjustable peg or a fixed exchange rate system. Though the classical gold standard regime provided a credible commitment mechanism before World War I, adherence to the nominal anchor provided by the fixed price of gold can be greatly improved upon by monetary authorities following credible rules in a fiat regime with flexible exchange rates.

NOTES

1. Theoretical developments in recent years have complicated the simple distinction between fixed and floating rates. In the presence of capital mobility, currency substitution, policy reactions and policy interdependence, floating rates no longer necessarily provide insulation from either real or monetary shocks (Bordo and Schwartz, 1989). Moreover, according to recent real business cycle approaches, there may be no relationship between the international monetary

regime and the transmission of real shocks (Baxter and Stockman, 1989). Nevertheless the comparison between regimes may shed light on these issues.

2. See, for example, Helpman and Razin (1979) and Helpman (1981).

3. One important caveat is that the historical regimes presented here do not represent clear examples of fixed and floating exchange rate regimes. The inter-war period does not represent a clear example of either a fixed or a floating rate regime. It comprises three regimes: a general floating rate system from 1919 to 1925, the gold exchange standard from 1926 to 1931 and a managed float to 1939. For a detailed comparison of the performances of these three regimes in the inter-war period, see Eichengreen (1991). We include this regime as a comparison with the other three more clear-cut cases. The Bretton Woods regime cannot be characterized as a fixed exchange rate regime throughout its history. The preconvertibility period was close to the adjustable peg envisioned by its architects, and the convertible period was close to a de facto fixed dollar standard. (Within the sample of seven countries, Canada floated from 1950 to 1961.) Finally, although the period since 1973 has been characterized as a floating exchange rate regime, at various times it has experienced varying degrees of management.

4. The period 1946–73, which includes the three years of transition from the Bretton Woods adjustable peg to the present floating regime, was also examined. The results are similar to those of the 1946–70 period.

5. Bordo (1993a) also presents data on seven other variables: money growth, nominal and real short-term and long-term interest rates and nominal and real exchange rates. Bordo and Schwartz (1994) shows the same data plus the government budget deficit relative to GDP for 14 additional countries.

6. The dispersion of inflation rates between countries was highest during the classical gold standard and to a lesser extent during the Bretton Woods convertible subperiod compared to the floating rate period and the mixed inter-war regime (Bordo, 1993a). This evidence is consistent with the traditional view of the operation of the classical price specie-flow mechanism and commodity arbitrage under fixed rates and insulation and greater monetary independence under floating rates.

7. Based on AR (1) regressions on CPI data. See Alogoskoufis and Smith (1991), Eichengreen (1993) and Bordo (1993b).

8. The Bretton Woods regime also exhibited the lowest dispersion of output variability between countries of any regime, with the inter-war regime the highest (Bordo, 1993a). The lower dispersion of output variability under Bretton Woods may reflect conformity between countries' business fluctuations, created by the operation of the fixed exchange rate regime (Bordo and Schwartz, 1989).

9. See Bayoumi and Eichengreen (1994).

10. The approach followed was originally developed by Blanchard and Quah (1989) and extended by Bayoumi and Eichengreen (1994). Restrictions on the VAR identify an aggregate demand disturbance, which is assumed to have only a temporary impact on output and a permanent impact on the price level, and an aggregate supply disturbance, which is assumed to have a permanent impact on both prices and output. Overidentifying restrictions, namely that demand shocks are positively correlated and supply shocks are negatively correlated with prices, can be tested by examining the impulse response functions to the shocks.

11. The dispersion of demand shocks across countries, as measured by the GNP weighted standard deviation of the individual country shocks around the G-7 aggregate, reveals very little difference between the gold standard and the post-World War II regimes, with the convertible Bretton Woods regime displaying the highest degree of convergence. Dispersion is much greater in the inter-war period. The dispersion of supply shocks is considerably greater during the gold standard and the inter-war periods than in any of the post-World War II regimes (Bordo, 1993a).

12. It is doubtful that the monetary regime had any connection with the different real growth rate performances across regimes, especially the link recently posited between the Bretton Woods arrangements and Europe's 'golden age' (Bretton Woods Commission, 1994; Eichengreen, 1994). At best, the Bretton Woods arrangements may have contributed to postwar growth by being part of the overall package creating political and economic stability in the postwar era – 'the Pax Americana', created in turn in reaction to the chaos of the inter-war period and

World War II. In this view, rapid postwar growth represented a 'catching up' by the European nations and Japan from low levels of per capita output compared to that of the leading industrial country, the USA. The 'catching up' occurred through these nations, encouraged by the USA, adopting the best practice technology of the leader and hence growing at a much more rapid rate (Abramowitz, 1986).

13. See, for example, Kenen (1994) and Bretton Woods Commission (1994).

REFERENCES

Abramowitz, Moses (1986), 'Catching Up, Forging Ahead and Falling Behind', *Journal of Economic History*, June **46**(2), 385–406.

Alogoskoufis, George S. and Ronald Smith (1991), 'The Phillips Curve, the Persistence of Inflation and the Lucas Critique: Evidence from Exchange-Rate Regimes', *American Economic Review*, December, 1254–75.

Barro, Robert J. and David B. Gordon (1983), 'Rules, Discretion and Reputation in a Model of Monetary Policy', *Journal of Monetary Economics*, **12**, 101–21.

Baxter, Marianne and Alan C. Stockman (1989), 'Business Cycles and the Exchange-Rate Regime: Some International Evidence', *Journal of Monetary Economics*, **23**, May, 377–400.

Bayoumi, Tamin and Barry Eichengreen (1994), 'Economic Performance Under Alternative Exchange Rate Regimes: Some Historical Evidence', in Peter Kenen, Francesco Papadia and Fabrizio Saccomani (eds), *The International Monetary System*, Cambridge: Cambridge University Press, pp. 257–97.

Blanchard, Olivier and Danny Quah (1989), 'The Dynamic Effects of Aggregate Demand and Aggregate Supply Disturbances', *American Economic Review*, September, 655–73.

Bordo, Michael D. (1981), 'The Classical Gold Standard: Some Lessons for Today', *Federal Reserve Bank of St Louis Review*, **63** (May), 2–17.

Bordo, Michael D. (1984), 'The Gold Standard: The Traditional Approach', in Michael D. Bordo and Anna J. Schwartz (eds), *A Retrospective on the Classical Gold Standard, 1821–1931*, Chicago: University of Chicago Press.

Bordo, Michael D. (1993a), 'The Gold Standard, Bretton Woods and Other Monetary Regimes: A Historical Appraisal', *Federal Reserve Bank of St Louis Review*, **75**(2) (March/April), 123–91.

Bordo, Michael D. (1993b), 'The Bretton Woods International Monetary System: An Historical Overview', in Michael D. Bordo and Barry Eichengreen (eds), *A Retrospective on the Bretton Woods System*, Chicago: University of Chicago Press.

Bordo, Michael D. and Finn E. Kydland (1996), 'The Gold Standard as a Commitment Mechanism', in Tamin Bayoumi, Barry Eichengreen and Mark Taylor (eds), *Modern Perspectives on the Gold Standard*, Cambridge: Cambridge University Press.

Bordo, Michael D. and Anna J. Schwartz (1989), 'Transmission of Real and Monetary Disturbances Under Fixed and Floating Rates', in James A. Dorn and William A. Niskanen (eds), *Dollars, Deficits and Trade*, Boston: Kluwer Academic Publishers, pp. 237–58.

Bordo, Michael D. and, Anna J. Schwartz (1996), 'The Operation of the Specie Standard: Evidence for Core and Peripheral Countries, 1880–1990', in Barry Eichengreen and Jorge Braga de Macedo (eds), *Historical Perspectives on the Gold Standard: Portugal and the World*, London: Routledge Publishers.

Bretton Woods Commission (1994), *Bretton Woods: Looking to the Future. Commission Report. Staff Review. Background Papers*, Washington, DC.

Eichengreen, Barry (1991), 'The Comparative Performance of Fixed and Flexible Exchange Rate Regimes: Inter-war Evidence', in Niel Thygesen *et al.* (eds), *Business Cycles: Theories, Evidence and Analysis*,London: Macmillan, pp. 229–72.

Eichengreen, Barry (1992), *Golden Fetters: The Gold Standard and the Great Depression, 1919–1939*, Oxford: Oxford University Press.

Eichengreen, Barry (1993), 'Epilogue: Three Perspectives on the Bretton Woods System', in Michael D. Bordo and Barry Eichengreen (eds), *A Retrospective on the Bretton Woods System*, Chicago: University of Chicago Press, pp. 621–57.

Eichengreen, Barry (1994), 'Institutions and Economic Growth: Europe After World War-II', Centre For Economic Policy Research Working Paper No. 973, June.

Feldstein, Martin and James Stock (1994), 'The Use of a Monetary Aggregate to Target Nominal GDP', in N.G. Mankiw (ed.), *Monetary Policy*, Chicago: University of Chicago Press.

Friedman, Milton (1960), *A Program for Monetary Stability*. New York: Fordham University Press.

Giovannini, Alberto (1989), 'How Do Fixed-Exchange-Rate Regimes Work? Evidence From the Gold Standard, Bretton Woods and the EMS', in Marcus Miller, Barry Eichengreen and Richard Portes (eds), *Blueprints for Exchange Rate Management*, Center for Economic Policy Research, pp. 13–41.

Helpman, Elhanan (1981), 'An Exploration in the Theory of Exchange Rate Regimes', *Journal of Political Economy*, October, 865–90.

Helpman, Elhanan and Assaf Razin (1979), 'Towards a Consistent Comparison of Alternative Exchange Rate Systems', *Canadian Journal of Economics*, August, 394–409.

Kenen, Peter B. (1994), *Managing the World Economy: Fifty Years After Bretton Woods*, Washington, DC: Institute for International Economics.

Kydland, Finn E. and Edward Prescott (1977), 'Rules Rather than Discretion: The Inconsistency of Optimal Plans', *Journal of Political Economy*, **85**, 473–91.

Leijonhufvud, Alex (1984), 'Constitutional Constraints on the Monetary Power of Government', in Richard B. McKenzie (ed.), *Constitutional Economics*, Lexington, Mass.: Lexington Books, pp. 95–107.

McCallum, Bennett (1988), 'Robustness Properties of a Rule for Monetary Policy', *Carnegie–Rochester Conference Series on Public Policy*, **10**, (Autumn) 173–203.

Meltzer, Allan (1987), 'Limits of Short-Run Stabilization Policy', *Economic Inquiry*, January, 1–14.

5. Choice of target for monetary policy

Bennett T. McCallum

INTRODUCTION

Recent years have witnessed an upsurge of interest in issues regarding targets for monetary policy. This upsurge has occurred among not only academics but also practitioners, including central bankers. Indeed a number of central banks have assumed the responsibility of meeting explicitly specified targets for national inflation rates, targets that are serious in the sense that failures to meet them will result in significant losses of resources or prestige for the relevant central bank and/or its governor. Prominent examples are provided by current arrangements (as of April 1995) pertaining to the Bank of England, the Bank of Canada and the Reserve Bank of New Zealand.

Also contributing to the upsurge in interest is the possibility of European monetary unification. If a single currency and a unified central bank are created, it will be necessary to devise operational means for achieving the goal of low inflation that is expressed in the Maastricht Treaty. The very topic of monetary unification raises the issue from another perspective, moreover, since unification represents an extreme case of a fixed exchange rate arrangement, which is one form of a monetary policy target.[1]

A major reason for this upsurge has been a growing recognition of the desirability of a 'nominal anchor' that would keep inflation from getting out of hand and perhaps be helpful in escaping or lessening the inflationary bias that characterizes monetary policy when conducted in a so-called 'discretionary' fashion.[2] But various different nominal anchors are possible, so the issue naturally arises as to which target variable is the most desirable. Is it best, for example, to focus upon the price level, a monetary aggregate, nominal GDP or a foreign exchange rate? Furthermore it needs to be considered whether the target path should be of the growth rate or growing level type.[3] In other words, should past target misses be treated as irrelevant bygones or should they be treated as signals indicating that the target variable needs to be brought back to a prespecified path?

In actuality, the three examples of England, Canada and New Zealand all involve inflation rate targets: that is, ones in which the growth rate of the price level serves as the target variable. But several scholars have argued that nominal GDP (or some related variable) would be a better choice than the price level, whereas others have contended that targets should be of the growing level rather than the growth rate type. And of course the adoption of any of these targets for a domestic variable presupposes that a fixed exchange rate has been rejected in favour of one that floats to a substantial extent.

This chapter is intended to provide an analysis of these issues. It will begin by discussing the function of a target variable and by emphasizing the importance of focusing monetary policy upon some nominal target. Next it will briefly outline the relevant considerations for choosing between floating and fixed exchange rates. Then the growth rate versus growing level issue is considered and finally the choice among domestic target variables.

PRELIMINARIES

Because terminological usage is not the same for all writers, it may be useful to begin with a statement of what is meant, in this chapter, by a monetary policy target. In particular, targets need to be distinguished from instruments, indicators and goals. An instrument variable, in our terminology, is one that can be directly or accurately manipulated on a day-to-day basis by the central bank. In practice, most actual central banks use some short-term interest rate in this capacity, although it would be possible to use instead some measure of bank reserves or the monetary base (currency plus total reserves). Then, at the other end of the spectrum, are goal variables, which represent the ultimate objectives of monetary policy. These are typically far from being directly controllable and are usually expressed in amorphous terms involving economic progress or the welfare of the nation's citizens. A target variable, by contrast, is an operational concept that is more closely related to goals than is any potential instrument, but which is itself not directly controllable. Thus the idea of a target-oriented strategy is that a central bank will manipulate its instrument on a day-to-day or week-to-week basis so as to keep its target variable close to some desired path on a longer-term (for example, quarter-to-quarter) basis so as to achieve the best feasible performance in terms of ultimate goals. Not all central banks employ explicit target variables, but in what follows we shall take the desirability of doing so as given.

The distinction vis-à-vis indicator variables is easier to describe. Indicators are supposed to provide policy makers with some useful information but are not intended to be kept on desired paths. Keeping its target variable on a specified path is, by contrast, an overriding objective of the central bank when operating with a target-oriented strategy.

Considerable agreement has been reached in recent years concerning the importance of having some nominal variable – that is, one that is measured in monetary units such as dollars, pounds or yen – as the principal target variable. Since virtually all of a nation's nominal variables grow rapidly when inflation rates are high, keeping a nominal target variable on a reasonable growth path will serve to prevent excessive inflation. If the central bank were, by contrast, to focus entirely on a real target, such as an unemployment rate or real output growth, there would be no guarantee that high inflation (or deflation!) rates would be avoided. There would be no 'nominal anchor'.

DOMESTIC VERSUS EXCHANGE RATE TARGETS

An extremely basic decision is whether a nation's monetary target variable is to involve a fixed value[4] for a foreign exchange rate. If, for example, a nation commits itself to maintaining a fixed rate of exchange between its currency and the DM, it will have already adopted its monetary target variable. There is no way of permanently maintaining a prespecified exchange rate except by dedicating monetary policy to that purpose. It might be possible to affect exchange rate pressures temporarily by means of fiscal adjustments, but on a sustained basis there is no way to keep an exchange rate fixed except by maintaining an average rate of monetary growth that yields an average inflation rate corresponding to that of the relevant foreign currency (appropriate account being taken of any trend growth in the real exchange rate).[5]

Let us quickly review, then, considerations relevant to a nation's choice between fixed and floating exchange rates. The clearest way to conceptualize the issue is to presume temporarily that any fixed rate arrangement to be considered would be of the extreme and pure type in which two or more nations share a common currency – that is, use the same money. Now there are certainly advantages of having a common money, a common medium of exchange, over any given area, whether or not it is an area that conforms to a single political entity. These advantages are the same ones as are generally recognized as accruing to a monetary economy as opposed to one of the non-monetary type. In particular, the use of a common medium of exchange throughout an economy drastically reduces the time and resources that would be needed to find trading partners for market exchanges of goods and services if these had to be conducted by barter (with its requirement of a 'double coincidence of wants'). Also important are the efficiencies of having a single generally accepted medium of account, so that only $n-1$ prices need to be quoted for n goods, rather than $n(n-1)/2$. And a final element of efficiency in the exchange process is provided by having the medium of account be the same as the medium of exchange, thereby eliminating the need for one extra calculation by each party to an exchange. These advantages of a monetized economy are simple and familiar, but are nevertheless of enormous importance, as the mere contemplation of barter demonstrates. Thus it is the case that there is virtually no support whatsoever for the possibility of using different moneys – with a floating rate of exchange – in different neighbourhoods of London (such as Kensington and Mayfair) or even in different counties of England (such as Kent and Sussex) or different states in the USA. But it is useful to note that these advantages are entirely microeconomic in nature. They involve, that is, efficiency gains reflecting the avoidance of wasted time and other resources in the process of exchange. They depend ultimately upon uncertainties relating to specific details of the exchange process.

The advantages of different moneys and floating exchange rates are, by contrast, entirely macroeconomic in nature. In particular, they permit monetary policy to be relatively restrictive in some areas and stimulative in others. The stock of money can be growing rapidly in the UK but slowly in Germany, for example. With a common currency this discrepancy would not be possible, for the comparative monetary stringency in Germany would tend to raise interest rates there and attract financial flows away from the UK. But, with distinct currencies, it is possible because of expected exchange rate depreciation for different interest rates to obtain in the two areas without inducing any substantial volume of financial flows. Consequently monetary policy actions can be used to offset shocks that impinge upon one area but not the other. The real effects of such actions will be temporary, but may be of considerable importance nevertheless – as the UK experience of 1992–3 demonstrated.[6] In sum, with floating exchange rates a nation has the possibility of using monetary policy to combat business cycle fluctuations on a short-run basis. In addition, it also has the ability to select its own trend (or long-run) inflation rate.[7] These two basic advantages of a floating exchange rate are both macroeconomic in nature. To summarize, then, a common currency arrangement offers microeconomic efficiency gains, whereas different currencies with a floating exchange rate provide scope for superior macroeconomic performance.

The foregoing argument has not referred to the possibility of different currencies with a fixed exchange rate, but this case can be analysed by observing that, if the exchange rate is permanently fixed, it amounts to an inferior modification of the common currency arrangement. It is slightly inferior to a common currency because the need to make currency conversions implies that the potential microeconomic efficiencies are not fully obtained. But the advantages of a fixed rate, relative to one that floats, are still entirely microeconomic in nature.

This last contention, it will be noted, flies in the face of the frequently expressed idea that a fixed rate is a useful anti-inflationary device, one that can bring discipline to a nation's monetary affairs. In that regard, it is of course true that a nation that keeps a fixed exchange rate with a non-inflationary nation must itself be non-inflationary in its policy stance. But the same non-inflationary stance would be available to it with a floating rate; by adopting a suitable monetary policy rule the nation can have whatever long run average inflation rate it chooses. The alleged disciplinary advantages of a fixed rate are all essentially political, not economic, in nature. That does not make them unimportant, but it implies that they have no proper place in an economic analysis of the issue.

One more apparent gap in our argument is that nothing has thus far been said regarding an exchange rate that is fixed temporarily, rather than permanently. Does not such an arrangement offer the possibility of some incomplete advantages of both types, microeconomic efficiencies and macroeconomic flexibility? Such might be the case if an arrangement of this type were truly feasible, but my argument is that temporary fixity is not viable. The basic reason is the one identified long ago by Milton Friedman, namely that temporary fixity is a self-destructive arrangement because it virtually invites speculative attacks. In Friedman's words,

> because the exchange rate is changed infrequently and only to meet substantial difficulties, a change tends to come well after the onset of difficulty, to be postponed as long as possible, and to be made only after substantial pressure on the exchange rate has accumulated. In consequence, there is seldom any doubt about the direction in which an exchange rate will be changed [if at all]. In the interim between the suspicion of a possible change in the rate and the actual change, there is every incentive to sell the country's currency if a devaluation is expected or buy if [a revaluation] is expected [thereby adding to the pre-existing pressure for a change]. (Milton Friedman (1953), *The Case for Flexible Exchange Rates: Essays in Positive Economics*, Chicago: University of Chicago Press, p. 164)

The wisdom of this observation has been borne out, one might reasonably conclude, by the breakdown in 1992 and 1993 of the exchange rate mechanism of the European Monetary System. My position, then, is that an exchange rate target (that is, a fixed exchange rate) is economically appropriate for a nation only if it would yield microeconomic efficiencies that outweigh the macroeconomic flexibility afforded by a floating rate. For two nations that are geographically adjacent and whose citizens conduct many transactions with each other, such as Belgium and Luxembourg, a common currency may be advantageous especially if one of the nations is small. Indeed it is possible that a single-currency monetary union involving several nations (such as those of Europe) could be desirable on strictly economic grounds.[8] But for many nations it will be the case that a fixed exchange rate is not the best nominal anchor. Furthermore currency unions themselves need to select nominal internal variables for guidance of their own monetary policy – each one needs to decide which variable to go for. Consequently our discussion will continue under the presumption that it pertains to an economy with a floating exchange rate.

GROWTH RATES VERSUS GROWING LEVELS

At this point we turn to the question of whether it is preferable to have a growth rate target or one of the growing levels type. It might seem somewhat strange to be discussing this issue before settling on the identity of the variable whose growth rate or (growing) level is to be selected, but the former question is in fact a simpler one and the same basic considerations are applicable whichever variable is settled upon. In particular, the weakness of the growth rate choice is that it will, by treating past target misses as bygones, introduce a random-walk or 'unit root' component into the time series processes for all nominal variables, including the price level (whatever index is chosen) or its logarithm. Thus there will be a possibility that the price level will drift arbitrarily far away from any given value (or path) as time passes, implying considerable uncertainty as to the value that will obtain in the distant future (for example, 50 years from the present).

By contrast, the principal disadvantage with a levels-type target path is that the target variable will be forced back towards the preset path after any disturbance has driven it away, even if the effect of the disturbance itself is of a permanent nature. Since any such action entails general macroeconomic stimulus or restraint, this type of targeting procedure would apparently induce extra cyclical variation in demand conditions which will imply extra variability in real output if price level stickiness prevails. And variability in output and other real aggregative variables is probably more costly to society (in terms of human welfare) than variability in the price level about a constant or slowly growing path. Now it is not clear that fully permanent shocks are predominant, but most time series analysis seems to suggest that the effects of shocks are typically quite long-lasting – indeed virtually indistinguishable from fully permanent. Consequently it would seem preferable not to drive the nominal target variable back to a preset path, or at least not to do so quickly. In other words, it seems preferable to adopt a nominal target of the growth rate type, rather than the levels type.

One reason for reaching the above conclusion is that very few economic transactions are based on 50-year planning horizons. A typical 'long-lasting' arrangement might be more like 20 years in duration. But price level uncertainty 20 years into the future would not be terribly large even if the log of the price level were to behave as a pure random walk with zero drift. Assuming that the random, unpredictable component at the quarterly frequency has a variance of 0.00002 – roughly the value for the USA over the period 1954–91 – a 95 per cent confidence interval for the log price level 20 years ahead would be within 8 per cent (plus or minus) of the current value. This, it is suggested, represents a small degree of uncertainty in comparison with the magnitudes that have prevailed over the 1960s, 1970s and 1980s, essentially because the drift or trend rate has been non-zero and uncertain.

Even so, it might be possible to do even better by adopting a target that is a weighted average of the growth rate and growing levels type. In a study of targeting procedures for Japan, it was found that a weighted average target that gives a weight of 80 per cent to a growth rate path and 20 per cent to a growing levels value yields quite desirable results.[9] Specifically, in the relevant simulations typical deviations from the growth rate target path are almost as small as when growth rate targets are aimed for, and the deviations from a growing levels path are also reasonably small. In particular there is a distinct tendency for the simulated nominal values to return to the growing levels path, rather than drifting away arbitrarily as when pure growth rate targeting is adopted.

CHOICE OF NOMINAL VARIABLE

Finally we turn to the selection of the nominal domestic variable to be targeted. In my own work,[10] I have generally taken nominal GNP (or GDP) or some related measure of nominal aggregate spending to be an appropriate choice. But clearly this choice warrants careful consideration, for some analysts would favour traditional monetary aggregates (such as M1, M2 or M3) whereas others would recommend direct targeting of the price level, or perhaps some weighted average of price level and real output variables. Also, as previously mentioned, the central banks of Canada, New Zealand and the UK have in practice favoured direct price level targets (in growth rate form).

A major reason for favouring GDP over the M1–M3 monetary aggregates is that one can be confident that keeping its growth close to the targeted value will result in inflation close to its desired rate on average, that is, over a decade or more. This is so because the average long-run growth rate of real output is predictable to within approximately ± 0.5 percentage points per annum.[11] The UK's real output growth rate may vary from 6 per cent to negative values over a year or so, but over the next decade it will almost certainly be quite close to 2 or 2.0 per cent. So keeping nominal GDP growing at 4.5 per cent will result in an average inflation rate of close to 2.5 percent, if one provisionally takes the latter to be the desired rate of inflation. With the monetary aggregates, by contrast, one must also take account of the growth rate of velocity, and the worldwide experience of the past 30 years has shown that these values can be mispredicted by several percentage points, even over a decade or so, because of the uneven pace of technological and regulatory change in the payments industry.[12]

But what about direct price level targeting, perhaps in its growth rate form? Such a target would, if successful, obviously offer tighter short-run control over the inflation rate. But it is nevertheless arguable that nominal GDP targeting would be preferable, even if long-run inflation control is the central bank's main goal, for three reasons. First, because the prices of goods and services evidently react more slowly than output in response to monetary actions,[13] cycling and dynamic instability are more likely with a price level (or inflation) target. In other words, the problem of potential 'instrument instability', which would render the attempt entirely unsuccessful, is intensified. Second, the output-stabilizing properties of a smoothed path for nominal GDP are probably better than for a smoothed path of the price level. About this we cannot be certain, because the economics profession has a very poor understanding of the dynamic short-run interactions between nominal and real variables, that is, of aggregate supply or short-run Phillips curve behaviour, and of the magnitude and serial correlation properties of the various types of shocks that are of macroeconomic significance. But, furthermore, this poor understanding accounts for our third reason. It does so by suggesting that it is more difficult to devise a policy rule for achieving inflation targets than for achieving nominal GDP targets, because the former requires an understanding of the forces that determine the split of nominal GDP growth into its inflation and real growth components. When a central bank takes stimulative policy actions, it can predict more accurately when and by how much nominal GDP will rise than it can for the price level.

Some economists[14] have argued for a target that gives more weight to output movements and less to inflation than does a GDP target, which weights them equally.[15] But a strong counterargument is that choice of some putative 'optimal' weights again relies on knowledge that the profession does not possess. Indeed the optimal weights depend not only on knowledge of short-run aggregate supply or Phillips curve behaviour, but also on the social costs of inflation and output variability, about which there is substantial professional disagreement. To favour GDP targeting is not to claim that it is optimal, but instead that it would provide a simple and readily intelligible scheme that is likely to work at least moderately well under a wide variety of conditions.

A practical objection to GDP targeting is that national income statistics are not produced often or quickly enough, and are significantly revised after their first release. But the essence of the approach is to use some reasonably comprehensive measure of nominal spending; it need not be GDP or GNP. Other measures could readily be developed on the basis of price and quantity indices that are reported more often and more promptly. It might even be possible to devise a monthly measure that was conceptually more satisfactory than GDP, by making the price index more closely tailored to public perceptions of inflation and/or by using quantity measures that treat government output more appropriately. In any event, in practice actual central banks base their action on expected future target misses, not past values.

CONCLUSION

In summary, this chapter has argued, first, that monetary targets should be nominal and, second, that any decision to use an exchange rate target should be made on microeconomic or political grounds (because a domestic variable would be preferable from a macroeconomic perspective). Among the various contenders for the domestic variable to be targeted, some measure of aggregate spending such as nominal GDP seems clearly preferable to monetary aggregates and arguably preferable to a price level index. A growth rate version of the chosen variable, with past target misses treated as bygones, would probably be preferable to a growing levels version, but a weighted average of the two could be better still. Most of these conclusions are based on judgments that are not capable of 'proof' because the economics profession does not possess adequate knowledge to permit any degree of certainty. This absence of knowledge itself should be taken into account, and in my judgment provides one of the reasons for favouring a nominal spending target. In that regard, however, it must be acknowledged that actual experiences with inflation targets have thus far been rather encouraging and that it would certainly be undesirable for target variables to be changed frequently.

NOTES

1. Monetary unification implies a single currency and a single central bank (perhaps with national 'branches'), whereas a system of fixed exchange rates permits separate currencies and central banks in the participating nations. But with 'irrevocably' fixed exchange rates, the national central banks have very little autonomy (as is discussed below, pp. 60–62).
2. The inflationary bias of discretionary (that is, period-by-period) policy making was explained in two classic articles: F.E. Kydland and E.C. Prescott, 'Rules Rather than Discretion: The Inconsistency of Optimal Plans', *Journal of Political Economy*, **85** (1977) and R.J. Barro and D.B. Gordon, 'A Positive Theory of Monetary Policy in a Natural-Rate Model', *Journal of Political Economy*, **91** (1983). A textbook exposition appears in Chapter 16 of B.T. McCallum, *Monetary Economics: Theory and Policy*, London and New York: Macmillan, 1989.
3. To illustrate the difference, suppose that the target path rises on average at a rate of 3 per cent per year and that the target value is exceeded by 1 per cent in some period. Then the desired growth rate in the next period would be 3 per cent with a growth rate target but only 2 per cent if the target path is of the growing level type.
4. Or a fixed *path* for an exchange rate, which is analytically similar in most respects.
5. If a fixed path is chosen, the effect of the chosen rate of depreciation must also be taken into account.
6. After leaving the ERM in September 1992, the UK was able to pursue a more expansionary monetary policy than before and consequently came out of the recession more quickly than other European nations.
7. The latter could also be accomplished with a fixed exchange rate path.
8. In the case of Europe, it seems likely that political objectives have played a major role in spurring the move towards monetary integration.
9. See B.T. McCallum, 'Specification and Analysis of a Monetary Policy Rule for Japan', Bank of Japan, *Monetary and Economic Studies*, **11** (1993). The growth rate and growing level targets

are $x_t^{**} = x_{t-1} + 0.01468$ and $x_t^* = x_{t-1}^* + 0.01468$, respectively, where 0.01468 represents a 6 per cent per annum rate expressed in logarithmic units for quarter-year periods. The weighted average target for period t is then $0.8x_t^{**} + 0.2x_t^*$.

10. These studies include 'Robustness Properties of a Rule for Monetary Policy', *Carnegie–Rochester Conference Series on Public Policy*, **29**, (1988); 'Targets, Indicators and Instruments of Monetary Policy', in W.S. Haraf and P. Cagan (eds), *Monetary Policy for a Changing Financial Environment*, Washington, DC: AEI Press, 1990; 'Could a Monetary Base Rule Have Prevented the Great Depression?', *Journal of Monetary Economics* **26** (1990); 'Monetary Policy Rules and Financial Stability' in K. Sawamoto, Z. Nakajima and H. Taguchi (eds), *Financial Stability in a Changing Environment*, London and New York: Macmillan, 1995, and the publication cited in note 9.

11. That the long-run average growth rate of real output is independent of average growth rates of nominal variables – a proposition known as the 'natural rate hypothesis' – is agreed by a great majority of macroeconomic researchers, be they Keynesian, monetarist or new classical in their beliefs.

12. Much has been made of the fact that M2 velocity has shown no upward or downward trend in the USA since about 1960. But prior to that date it had experienced several periods of distinct trends: see page 644 of M. Friedman and A.J. Schwartz, *A Monetary History of the United States 1867–1960*, Princeton: Princeton University Press, 1963; and in other nations its recent behaviour has not been trendless. In short, there is little if any reason to be confident of future M2 velocity trends.

13. This is documented in a host of papers, including the contribution of L.J. Christiano, M. Eichenbaum and C. Evans, 'The Effects of Monetary Policy Shocks: Some Evidence from the Flow of Funds', National Bureau of Economic Research (NBER) W.P. 4699 (1994).

14. A prominent example is R.E. Hall, 'Monetary Policy with an Elastic Price Standard', *Price Stability and Public Policy*, Kansas: Federal Reserve Bank of Kansas City (1984).

15. This statement presumes a logarithmic formulation: the log of nominal GDP equals the (equal weighted) sum of the log of real GDP and the log of the GDP deflator. Logarithmic measures are appropriate because their movements correspond to percentage movements in the raw (unlogged) variables.

6. Money and interest rates

Geoffrey E. Wood[*]

The relationship between changes in the quantity (or in the growth rate of the quantity) of money and the behaviour of interest rates is one that has interested economists from at least the middle of the eighteenth century. Indeed the principles were established by 1802, when Henry Thornton's *An Enquiry into the Nature and Effects of the Paper Credit of Great Britain* was first published. Subsequent authors have added various refinements to the structure inherited from Thornton and some other eighteenth- and early nineteenth-century writers, but there has been no successful challenge to its fundamental conclusions. This chapter sets out these conclusions, displays a little evidence in support of them and (very briefly) discusses some elaborations. But first some preliminary definitions are necessary.

DEFINITIONS

It is essential to keep certain distinctions in mind throughout what follows. The first is the distinction between nominal and real interest rates. Nominal interest rates are what is generally quoted in financial markets; they tell (for example) how much money will be received in return for lending a sum of money over a certain period. Real interest rates are those nominal rates adjusted for inflation, so as to show the change in purchasing power expected to result from the transaction. They can be defined as the nominal rate minus the expected inflation rate over the period of the loan. This calculation reveals the rate of interest relevant for a savings or investment decision which is about to be made. For example, if the nominal rate is 10 per cent per annum and the expected inflation rate is 6 per cent per annum, the expected real rate is 4 per cent per annum. Notice that this definition is quite different from a very common method of calculating supposedly real interest rates. This latter method involves subtracting the inflation rate over some past period (the previous year, say) from the current nominal rate. This method of calculation, though easy,

[*] I am indebted to Forrest Capie and George Pedden for their comments on an earlier draft of this chapter.

tells what the real return from making the loan will be only by chance – only if next year's inflation is the same as last year's. The calculation is unlikely to be very misleading at low rates of inflation (say 3 per cent per annum or below) for at that level inflation tends to change slowly; but if it is not misleading, it is so only by a happy accident. (The realized, as opposed to expected, real return is calculated by subtracting the inflation rate over the period of the investment just past from the interest rate paid on that investment.)

It is also necessary to distinguish between once-for-all and continuous changes. A once-for-all change in the quantity of money moves it from one level to another; a continuous change moves it from one growth rate to another. A once-for-all change in the price level changes it from one level to another; a continuous change in the price level is inflation.

Finally, in these preliminaries, a clarification. The interest rates we are concerned with are those determined in the market, *not* the rate or rates set by the central bank. This means that we need not get involved in the complication (minor but unnecessary) caused by central banks controlling monetary conditions by varying interest rates.

HISTORICAL BACKGROUND

Before providing an exposition in modern terms of the money–interest relationship, a brief review of what some classical economists said on the subject is useful; useful both because they wrote with great clarity and because it demonstrates the long-standing nature of the theory.

David Hume argued that interest rates were unaffected by monetary changes. The real rate, he maintained, is a real variable. While a monetary injection may for a time lower the real rate, that injection will ultimately raise prices and, via the effects of rising prices on loan demand, carry interest rates back to their previous level. Two quotations summarize first the channels of transmission, and then why interest rates must be restored to their original level. Hume assumed that the monetary injection was initially concentrated in the hands of potential lenders.

> The encrease of lenders above the borrowers sinks the interest; and so much the faster, if those, who have acquired those large sums, find ... no method of employing their money but by lending it at interest. But after this new mass of gold and silver has been digested, and has circulated through the whole state, affairs will soon return to their former situation...The whole money may still be in the state, and make itself felt by the encrease of prices: But [the resulting rise in the loan demand ensures that] the disproportion between the borrowers and lenders is the same as formerly, and consequently the high interest returns. (Hume, 1961, p. 58)

The real nature of interest rates, their other than temporary immunity to monetary phenomena, is explained succinctly, as follows:

> ... suppose, that by miracle every man in Great Britain should have five pounds slipt into his pocket in one night; this would much more than double the whole money that is at present in the kingdom; yet there would not ... be ... any variation in the interest ...That [a fall in interest] depends upon another principle; and must proceed from an encrease of industry and frugality, of arts and commerce. (Ibid., p. 51)

Henry Thornton (1802) added two qualifications to this. These were, first, that with inconvertible paper currency the money supply could rise without limit. Hence, if the nominal money supply could keep on growing faster than prices were rising, interest rates could be depressed by monetary actions. A second possibility was that the monetary injection would produce an increase in the stock of physical capital. This, he suggested, would follow if (since wages lagged prices) the owners of capital had a higher propensity to save than did the suppliers of labour. He did, however, consider this to be a theoretical curiosity.

David Ricardo forcefully rejected even that latter minor qualification to the real nature of the rate of interest:

> I believe ... that no amount of loans which the Bank might make, and no degree of lowness of interest at which it might choose to lend, would alter the permanent rate of interest in the market. Interest is regulated chiefly by the profits that may be made by the use of capital; it cannot be controlled by any bank [including the central bank], nor by any assemblage of banks. (1923, p. 280)

As he put it in his famous essay on 'The High Price of Bullion and Depreciation of Bank Notes' (1811), 'the rate of interest is regulated by the abundance or scarcity of that part of capital not consisting of money ... As the increase of bank notes does not add to this species of capital ... it cannot ... lower interest' (1923, pp. 32, 36). He conceded that the central bank could temporarily depress interest rates, but he stressed the transience of this effect: no central bank, despite its best efforts, could prevent rates from eventually returning to their real, equilibrium, level. He wrote:

> I do not dispute, that if the Bank were to bring a large additional sum of notes into the market, and offer them on loan, but that they would for a time affect the rate of interest ... but having done so ... the notes ... would [not] be retained unemployed by the borrowers; they would be sent into every market, and would everywhere raise the prices of commodities, till they were absorbed in the general circulation. It is only during the interval of the issues of the Bank, and their effect on prices, that we should be sensible of an abundance of money; interest would, during that interval, be under its natural level; but as soon as the additional sum of notes ... became absorbed in

the general circulation, the rate of interest would be high, and new loans would be demanded with as much eagerness as before the additional issues. (Ibid. p. 35)

In short,

> Reduction or Increase of the Quantity of Money always ultimately raises or lowers the Price of Commodities; when this is effected, the Rate of Interest will be precisely the same as before; it is only during the Interval, that is, before the Prices are settled at the new Rate, that the Rate of Interest is either raised or lowered. (Ibid., p. 45)

Another view, sometimes called Keynesian, is in pronounced contrast to that of these classical authors. It was set out with great clarity by Joan Robinson (1952) in her *The Rate of Interest and Other Essays*. She expounds it first by summarizing an argument she attributes to the *General Theory*, and then qualifying that argument. In her essay, 'The Generalisation of the General Theory', she writes (p. 73):

> When unemployment appears, the argument runs, money wages and prices fall. If the quantity of money is not reduced correspondingly, the existence of cash now redundant to the needs of active circulation causes the rate of interest to fall, and this process continues until the fall in interest rates has stimulated investment (or reduced thriftiness) sufficiently to restore full employment.

This argument plainly implies that a once-for-all change in the supply of money (relative to demand) has a permanent effect on the real rate of interest – a very sharp contrast to the views discussed above. Her main concern with the argument is not that conclusion, but rather the fear that because of 'a confident belief in the normal value of the rate of interest ... the rate of interest would refuse to fall' (p. 75). She admits that the expectations which produce this stickiness will gradually change, but they will change only slowly, so that 'the automatic corrective action of the rate of interest is condemned by its very nature to be too little and too late' (p. 76). Robinson's conclusion is that 'mere monetary management cannot preserve full employment' (p. 77). Note that there is no hint that monetary policy cannot permanently change the interest rate – only the fear that, because of sluggish expectations, leading perhaps to the liquidity trap, it cannot do enough.

In Robinson's essay entitled 'The Rate of Interest', this model of interest rate determination – liquidity preference – is elaborated. The first generalization is to recognize that there is a whole range of rates of interest, on different types of asset; these vary with their riskiness as compared to the rate on a risk-free bond, which in turn is determined by liquidity preference. Robinson next analyses an open market operation, but the attention here is on how expectations influence the extent to which such an operation, if carried out at the short end of the yield curve, feeds through to rates at the long end. At the end of her discussion she writes, 'to summarise: given the state of expectations, the long and short rates of interest both fall as the quantity of money increases relatively to national income' (p. 17). The only qualification admitted is the liquidity trap. Finally, there is a brief discussion in the same essay on 'A Cheap Money Policy'. On this she writes '[a] campaign by the monetary authorities to lower interest rates to counter unemployment, if successful, will stimulate activity' (p. 28). The qualification relates, however, not to fears that the effect of money on interest rates is inevitably transitory but rather to the possibility that either a cartel ('a gentleman's agreement'(p. 29)) or the liquidity trap will prevent rates being driven low enough.

In summary, the theory of the rate of interest that Robinson sets out is that it is basically determined in the money market, and can be manipulated by the monetary authorities. Whether or not that was a correct reading of Keynes, it was a popular one. It could scarcely be more different from the more traditional view, although it does have some points of contact so far as short-run analysis goes.

MONEY GROWTH AND INTEREST RATES

Set out in this section are the effects of a once-for-all shift from one steady rate of money growth to another. The effects of such a shift fall into three groups. There is first an impact effect, which may be a combination of Keynes's liquidity effect and a first-round loanable funds effect; then there is an income effect; finally there is an effect on price expectations. To simplify exposition it is assumed that the monetary change is unanticipated and that prices are sticky.

Consider first the pure liquidity effect. Here the only variable that can change to clear the money market is the nominal rate of interest; both income and prices are assumed to be constant. A simple money demand curve (Figure 6.1) can thus be used to illustrate what happens. Initially equilibrium is at R_1. The growth rate of nominal money now rises. The interest rate has to fall and, as there is not just a stock increase (in which case a once-for-all drop in interest rates would be sufficient), but an increased rate of change, interest rates will decline continually, ending their decline only if the money demand function becomes infinitely elastic at some positive rate (or at zero otherwise).

A second short-run effect, still retaining the rigid price and unchanging income assumptions, may also be important. This is the *loanable funds effect*. This arises because (nowadays) an increased supply of money comes through the banking system. Bank reserves rise as a result of the central bank's actions, there is an increase in supply of loanable funds and so a *drop* (once-for-all) in the interest rate.

So far, then, two relationships, both short-run, one inevitable and one possible but not inevitable, have been identified. The liquidity effect shows a relationship

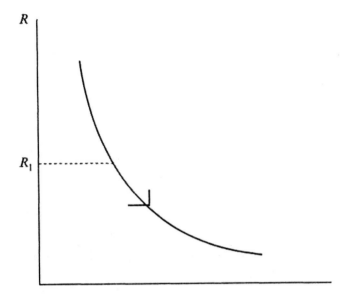

Figure 6.1   Pure liquidity effect

between the level of interest rates and the stock of money; or, alternatively, between the rate of change of the nominal interest rate and that of the quantity of money. From the liquidity effect, so long as the stock of nominal cash balances is growing, the nominal interest rate falls. In contrast, the loanable funds effect relates the level of the nominal interest rate to the acceleration in the quantity of money, because acceleration produces increased revenue to the money issuers and thereby an increase in credit. If both effects operate, an acceleration in the rate of growth of money would produce, first, a drop in the the interest rate, via the loanable funds effect, and then, via the liquidity effect, a falling interest rate for as long as the higher rate of money growth persists. This is set out in Figure 6.2, with the acceleration in money growth being at T_1. (So far, nominal and realized real interest rate movements have coincided, because neither the price level nor price level expectations has changed.)

Next we come to intermediate effects. By some mechanism – which can be Keynesian (lower interest rates), or of the type set out in Friedman and Schwartz (1982), where monetary expansion raises the prices of services relative to the price of the assets which supply the services – nominal income starts to rise. Assume, for the moment, that the entire effect is on real income. This rise in income will shift the money demand function of Figure 6.1 upwards, and thus raise interest rates again. How far will they rise? Back to their original level, for, until that is reached, there is a stimulus to income. So the second effect is

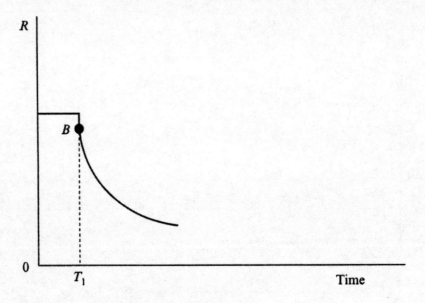

Figure 6.2   Loanable funds and liquidity effects

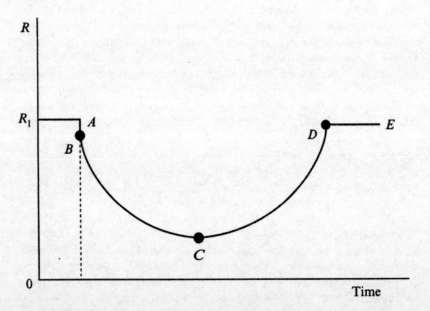

Figure 6.3a   Loanable funds, liquidity, and income effects

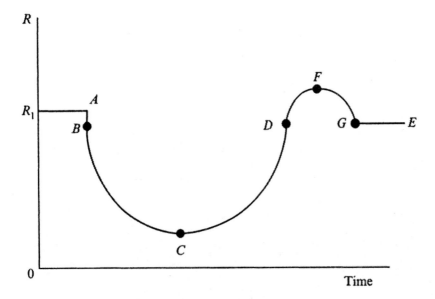

Figure 6.3b   Loanable funds, liquidity, and income effects with overshooting

an income effect which, via a rise in income, raises rates back to their original level. (Again, to this point it has been assumed that prices have not moved, so nominal and realized real rates coincide.)

Can one say anything about the path through time of this process, along the rudimentary lines of the path of the impact effects set out in Figure 6.2? One can. Consider Figure 6.3. It has been argued that rates first fall, and then rise to their original level. They need not, however, follow the path *ABCDE* with *AB* the loanable funds effect, *BC* the liquidity effect, and *CD* the income effect, as shown in Figure 6.3a, but rather a path with some degree of overshooting, such as *ABCDFGE* shown in Figure 6.3b. This is because income does not respond immediately to the monetary stimulus, so to attain its new and higher growth rate it has for a time to grow faster than the long-run rate. So the income effect is initially stronger than it is ultimately and hence interest rates may overshoot.[1]

PRICE EXPECTATIONS

So far no mention has been made of inflation, but a higher growth of money has been superimposed on an unchanged real economy. The real growth rate of the system has not changed. Higher money growth thus ends up producing

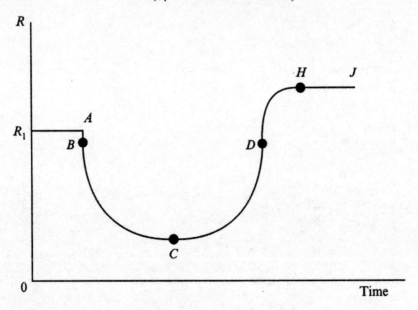

Figure 6.4   Loanable funds, liquidity, income, and inflation expectations effects

a rising price level, with the higher nominal income growth of the intermediate income effect decomposing into unchanged real growth plus inflation, as, for example, Wicksell (1907) described.

In these conditions, can the interest rate, as it has so far, be in equilibrium at its original level? If it did, the real rate of interest would have fallen. But nothing has changed to alter the equilibrium real yield. Hence, as the inflation becomes anticipated, nominal yields will rise until borrowers and lenders are in equilibrium once more. Initially the realized real yield may differ from the expected real yield while price expectations lag price performance. But, when expected inflation has caught up with actual inflation, expected real holding period yields will equal realized real yields, and both will be equal to the pre-monetary expansion non-inflationary real yield. A complete graph of the adjustment of interest rates to a change in the rate of money growth is shown in Figure 6.4.[2]

MONEY AND INTEREST RATES SUMMARIZED

The effect on the nominal rate of interest of a permanent change in the growth rate of the money stock comes in four stages. (Described below is an increase in the growth of money; for a decrease, simply reverse the directions of change of the interest rate.)

1. *Loanable funds effect*   The revenue accruing to money issuers, *if they use it to add to their holdings of assets*, lowers the nominal and real rates of interest.
2. *Liquidity effect*   So long as neither income nor the price level adjusts, the rate of interest falls, so as to clear the money market.
3. *Income effect*   Falling nominal and real interest rates lead to rising income; this pulls the interest rate up, only stopping when the rate of interest is at its original level. This always happens in the traditional theory. It may happen in the 'Keynesian' theory, in which case a further stimulus can be applied to lower rates again.
4. *Inflation expectations*   Nothing real has changed, so inflation starts as money growth continues, and the nominal rate rises until it has risen by the extent of the inflation rate.

Now, how are these results affected if all monetary fluctuations are transitory? The word 'transitory' can have two distinct meanings in this context and it is essential to separate them. It can mean that the change in the rate of growth of money is transitory, so that, after an upsurge, money growth returns to its previous rate. Alternatively, it can mean that the actual increase in the stock of money is temporary, so that, after an upsurge, there is a decline, until the money stock is back where it was before.

If money growth returns to its previous (by assumption non-inflationary) rate, then any inflation which results must be transitory. Hence the expected inflation (Fisher) effect is ultimately offset. The monetary increase drives the interest rate through the first three of the phases set out above. Interest rates end at the same level as before. There has been a once-for-all rise in the price level, and as a result the stock of real cash balances is unchanged. In short, the only permanent effect is on the price level.

What if the money stock first rises, and then returns to its previous level? The best way to see what happens here is to analyse it as two separate effects: first a rise in the money stock, and then a fall. A one-off rise would be as above: we would see effects 1 to 3, and then a once-for-all rise in the price level. There would then be a fall in the money stock, producing effects 1 to 3, but with their directions opposite to those so far described. Ultimately the economy would end up as it was before.

QUALIFICATIONS

A qualification relating to the real balance effect – the phenomenon of the rate of saving being affected by the stock of real cash balances – has already been discussed in note 1. The two qualifications discussed here relate to the source of the changed rate of money growth. The first was pointed out by J.S. Mill

(1848). He observed that if the growth of the money stock was produced by the exploitation of a gold discovery, the first effect would be on miners' wages, and on the prices of what they bought. Mill then went on to argue that, by the processes described above (pp. 69–71), this change in relative prices would be temporary, and the final effect would be, as usual, on the purchasing power of money. He also remarked explicitly in this context that, as none of the revenue arising from the issue of new money *need* be used to augment wealth, there need be no fall in the interest rate from what has been termed the loanable funds effect (see p. 72).

The second qualification originated with Lloyd Metzler (1951). He considered the consequences of a monetary expansion produced by a purchase from the private sector of common stock. This, he argued, changed the amount of securities in the hands of the private sector and, by thus changing the terms on which securities would be held, changed both the amount of money that sector would wish to hold and the rate of interest. This hypothesis gave rise to an extensive debate (see, for example, Wright, 1952; Habeler, 1952; Collery, 1960; Mundell, 1960; Horwich, 1962).

The crucial point in the debate was whether the *value* of securities in the private sector's hands would change as the result of such an operation. Metzler's critics argued it would not, as the value of the securities was equal to the present value of their expected after-tax income stream, and taxes would fall by an amount equal to the revenue the government was now receiving from the ownership of securities. In his reply to his critics, Metzler (1973) argued that taxes could not be capitalized sufficiently well to leave the value of securities unchanged, so his effect would remain, at least in part. Whether it does so is of course an empirical matter, but before turning to the evidence it should be noted, first, that open market operations are generally carried out between money and bonds, and the latter may not be net wealth in the hands of the private sector; and second, that it has been shown (for example, Wood, 1976), that, even without capitalization of taxes, the Metzler result need not hold in the long run when the effect of changes in the rate of interest on investment is incorporated.

Third, it should be observed that interest rates may be influenced by confidence, or lack of it, in a particular government or state. This is not caught fully by expectations of inflation if there is the possibility of default or of the currency being made inconvertible. In the eighteenth and nineteenth centuries, for example, the British government prided itself on its ability to borrow at lower rates than could some nations which were seen as more likely, or at any rate less unlikely, to default.

THE EVIDENCE

In this section evidence from three sources is presented. The first is Schwartz (1981), which drew on some of the work underlying Friedman and Schwartz

(1982). In that work one of the empirical relationships examined was that between interest rates and inflation. Did nominal rates rise with inflation, as the above theoretical discussion suggests? The period studied started in 1874. For a good part of the study, the effect was 'very much damped' (Schwartz, 1981, p. 13); 'In recent years, however, nominal rates of interest have begun to track the rate of price change more closely than at any time from 1874.' It is notable that this change came about as inflation became more variable, and thus more worth anticipating. People did not seem to bother incorporating it into expectations when prices rose and then fell; but when they rose continually, and at times quite rapidly, this was reflected in the interest rates which equilibrated borrowing and lending. This provides some support for the above theory.

Further support is provided by studies by Phillip Cagan. In two papers and a book (1966, 1969, 1972) he considered, first, whether the means of issue of money had any effect. He concluded that 'it makes no difference whether new money first enters into circulation through the banking system or not' (1969, p. 216): that, in other words, 'the effect of monetary changes on interest rates [was] largely unrelated to the means of issue' (ibid., p. 214). He also found that results allowing for lags 'suggested that the inverse effect of monetary growth on interest rates gradually disappears within the span of a business cycle (two to four years)' (ibid., p. 226). In terms of Figure 6.3a, this means that the time between point A and point D is some two to four years.

Evidence for Britain was provided in Mills and Wood (1988). These authors looked at the effects of monetary fluctuations on nominal interest rates over the years 1870 to 1913 and on a measure of real interest rates for the years 1972 to 1984. For the first period they found no evidence whatsoever of either a loanable funds or a liquidity effect. In other words, a rise in money growth did not seem to lower interest rates. (This apparent inconsistency with Cagan's above-noted results may have been produced by the combination of money fluctuations in this period in Britain being small and, as a result of data limitations, the unit of observation being one year.) With regard to real rates, despite much higher frequency data (monthly observations), no systematic effect of money on interest rates was found. (Again an apparent inconsistency with Cagan; but not a real one, for inflation was much higher in this period than in the one he studied, so inflationary expectations are likely to have been quicker to change.)

Finally it is worth commenting on the behaviour of interest rates in hyperinflations. These periods, of extraordinarily high inflation and similarly rapid money growth, were associated with rapidly rising rather than falling nominal interest rates. (See, for example, Cagan, 1969, for a classic discussion of some of these episodes.) Overall, then, the evidence suggests that, as has been argued from the time of David Hume, while monetary expansion may lower interest rates for a time, this effect is temporary. (And of course the same holds for the reverse effect, of a monetary contraction on interest rates.)

OVERVIEW AND CONCLUSION

This chapter has set out a theory of the effect of changes in the stock of money on market-determined interest rates. This theory, it has been argued, is of long standing, although it has been challenged from time to time. Examination of the evidence shows that these challenges have failed. The initial effect of a change in the stock of money on interest rates, if discernible in the data, produces a change in interest rates in the opposite direction to the monetary change. However, this change in interest rates is ultimately fully offset and interest rates return to their initial level. If the change is to the *rate of growth* of the money stock rather than to its level, a change in the rate of inflation results, leading to a proportionate change in nominal interest rates. In summary, the evidence is consistent with the body of theory which tells us that changes in monetary policy have no sustained effect on real rates of interest. Money has effects on nominal interest rates but, so far as expected real rates are concerned, its effects are temporary.

NOTES

1. Suppose that at this point money growth stopped; in other words, there has been an increase (once and for all) in the stock of money, *not* an increase in its growth rate. This increased money stock has been imposed on an unchanged real economy. Hence the ratio of nominal money to income is higher, with no change in the desire to hold money. The excess nominal money leads to a proportionate rise in prices, so that the stock of purchasing power held in money form – the stock of real money balances – is unchanged. The movement to this higher price level will lead to a temporary rise in interest rates above their original level, unless it is universally seen as a once-for-all rise in prices.

    This is discussed further below (p. 77) in the section on temporary monetary changes.
2. For the sake of expository simplicity the qualification to the Fisher effect, which was introduced by Mundell (1963) has been set aside. That author showed that, in the presence of a real balance effect, even a fully anticipated inflation reduces the real rate of interest. It does so via its effects on the stock of real cash balances, and thus on wealth. This was set aside because, as the effect works only via the stock of outside money, it is likely to be small. This theoretical preconception is confirmed by most investigations. Studies which do claim to find it significant have generally covered periods of accelerating and highly variable inflation, and the interpretation of their findings is, for that reason, not clear-cut.

BIBLIOGRAPHY

Cagan, P. (1966), 'Changes in the Cyclical Behaviour of Interest Rates', *Review of Economics and Statistics* (August Part III), 219–50.

Cagan, P. (1969), 'The Non-Neutrality of Money In the Long Run: A Discussion of the Critical Assumptions and Some Evidence', *Journal of Money, Credit and Banking*, **2**, 207–27.

Cagan, P. (1972), *The Channels of Monetary Influences on Interest Rates*, New York and London: Columbia University Press, for NBER.

Collery, A. (1960), 'A Note on the Saving–Wealth Relation and the Rate of Interest', *Journal of Political Economy*, **68**, (October).

Friedman, M. and A.J. Schwartz (1982), *Monetary Trends in the United States and the United Kingdom: Their Relation to Income, Prices and Interest Rates, 1867–1975*, Chicago and London: University of Chicago Press.

Haberler, G. (1962), 'The Pigou Effect Once More', *Journal of Political Economy*, **70** (April).

Horwich, G. (1962), 'Real Assets and the Theory of Interest', *Journal of Political Economy*, **70** (April).

Hume, D. (1961), *Writings on Economics*, ed. by Eugene Rotwein, Madison: University of Wisconsin Press.

Humphrey, T.M. (1983), 'Can the Central Bank Peg Real Interest Rates? A Survey of Classical and Neoclassical Opinion', Federal Reserve Bank of Richmond (September/October), 12–21.

Johnson, H.G. (1962), 'Monetary Theory and Policy', *American Economy Review*, **52** (June).

Metzler, L.A., (1951), 'Wealth, Saving and the Rate of Interest', *Journal of Political Economy*, **59** (April).

Metzler, L.A. (1973), 'The Structure of Taxes, Open Market Operations and the Rate of Interest', *Collected Papers of L.A. Metzler*, Cambridge, Mass.: Harvard University Press.

Mill, J.S. (1848), *Principles of Political Economy*, London: John W. Parker.

Mills, T.C., and G. E. Wood (1988), 'Interest Rates and the Conduct of Monetary Policy', in Walter Eltis and Peter Sinclair (eds), *Keynes and Economic Policy: The Relevance of the General Theory after 50 Years*, London: Macmillan.

Mundell, R.A. (1960), 'The Public Debt, Corporate Income Taxes and the Rate of Interest', *Journal of Political Economy*, **68** (December).

Ricardo, D. (1923), *Economic Essays by David Ricardo*; edited with introductory essay and notes by E.C.K. Gorner; 1966, New York: Augustus Kelly.

Robinson, J. (1952), *The Rate of Interest and Other Essays*, London: Macmillan.

Schwartz, Anna J. (1981), 'A Century of British Market Interest Rates 1874–1975', reprinted in F. Capie and G.E. Wood (eds) (1989), *Monetary Economics in the 1980s*, Basingstoke: Macmillan.

Thornton, H. (1802), *An Enquiry into the Nature and Effects of the Paper Credit of Great Britain*, edited with an Introduction by F.A. Hayek, 1939, New York: Rinehart & Company.

Wicksell, K. (1907), 'The Influence of the Rate of Interest on Prices', *Economic Journal*, **17**, 213–20.

Wood, G.E. (1976), 'Wealth, Saving and the Rate of Interest', *Bulletin of Economic Research* , **28** (2), November.

Wright, D.M., (1952), 'Professor Metzler and the Rate of Interest', *Journal of Political Economy*, **60** (June).

7. Money and real output

Robert H. Rasche

The perspective of the economics profession on the effect of money or a monetary impulse on real output is one of the most controversial issues in macroeconomics today. The controversial nature of this question is not new to the profession. During the past 50 years, even at those times when there existed a dominant or consensus position on the issue, there was always a strong minority opposition view. Some progress has been made both in theoretical research and empirical analysis that has narrowed the range of contention. At the present time there appears to be general support among economists and in the assumptions or implications of theoretical macroeconomic models that in the long run there are no substantial positive effects on real output or real output growth from a monetary expansion. The magnitude of short-run effects and their duration remains hotly disputed.

This chapter is structured to review the evolution of professional opinion and research over the past 50 years on the question of how and why changes in the nominal money stock or its rate of growth affect real output. The dominant perspective at the beginning of this period was that money and/or monetary policy was essentially completely benign with respect to real output and almost every other variable of macroeconomic importance. This view reflected the experience of the Great Depression and the theoretical framework proposed by Keynes in the *General Theory* as popularized by his disciples both in Europe and North America. In the aftermath of World War II, the dominant professional view was that monetary policy should focus on maintaining low and stable nominal interest rates to minimize the costs of financing and managing the large accumulations of public debt that had been incurred in the war effort. This view found support in theoretical macroeconomic models which assumed a fixed price level and empirical research results which alleged that the aggregate demand for goods and services was quite inelastic with respect to interest rates. Coincidentally, after demobilization, observed inflation rates in Europe and North America were low and inflation was not regarded as a major public policy problem.

In the late 1950s and early 1960s economists realized that theoretical and empirical models that started with an assumption of fixed nominal wages or a fixed price level did not provide a framework adequate to analyse the contemporaneous economic environment. Further, research on the Great Depression by Friedman and Schwartz provided an alternative interpretation which argued that, at least in the USA, monetary policy was a major contributing factor to the severity of that contraction. In this environment, the empirical analysis by Phillips of wage inflation and unemployment in the UK provided a needed modification to the prevailing macroeconomic paradigm.

The 'Phillips curve', at least as imported into the USA and incorporated into the existing macroeconomic models, provided an empirical framework with which to address the question of how monetary shocks are distributed between real output and inflation. The notion introduced into both theoretical and empirical models with the Phillips Curve was of a permanent 'trade-off' between inflation and either unemployment or real output growth. In this context, policy makers were seen as facing the unpleasant task of choosing a lower inflation rate at the cost of a higher level of unemployment or a lower rate of real output growth. The short-run terms of this trade-off were measured at different magnitudes from country to country, but for the USA the immediate response of any policy to change the rate of inflation implied a substantial change in the opposite direction of real output growth. Alternatively interpreted, a monetary stimulus was seen as producing substantial positive effects on real output in the short run, with little immediate increase in inflation. Over a longer response horizon, such as two to three years, empirical models incorporating this framework implied that such a monetary stimulus would have larger effects on the inflation rate and the initial real output response would be attenuated, but would remain positive indefinitely. In the jargon of the macroeconomic modelling profession, the real output impact multiplier for a nominal money shock was seen as positive, but after some time the dynamic multipliers become smaller as the real output response is dissipated. The impact multiplier of a nominal money shock on inflation was seen as close to zero, but the dynamic multipliers become appreciably positive with the passage of time.

This conception of the response of real output to a nominal money shock prevailed as the dominant paradigm among the economics profession for only a short period of time, though it is still influential in political economy analyses. Its demise is attributable to three factors. First, an alternative empirical analysis to the prevailing aggregate demand–Phillips curve structure appeared. This research initially was conducted at the Federal Reserve Bank of St. Louis and became known as the Andersen–Jordan equation and the Andersen–Carlson macroeconomic model. Initially the most controversial aspect of this research was the implied responses of real output and inflation to fiscal (particularly tax) policy shocks, but the more enduring implication concerned the response of real output to monetary policy shocks. The Andersen–Carlson model contained a short-run trade-off between inflation and real output such as that suggested by the Phillips curve, but it suggested that this trade-off was transitory. Over a horizon of several years, the response of real output to a change in the growth rate of the nominal money stock completely dissipated and the only permanent effect on the economy of such a stimulus was an increase in the rate of inflation.

The second factor contributing to revisionist thinking regarding the effect of monetary shocks on real output was empirical research on the Phillips curve itself. The negative relationship between inflation and unemployment proved ephemeral in light of the economic history of the 1960s. The only way that empirical studies were able to reproduce the Phillips curve relationship consistently was by adding more and more variables to the estimated relationship: in short the Phillips curve proved to be 'shifty', and the postulated trade-off between inflation and unemployment highly unstable. This is illustrated in Figure 7.1, where quarterly observations on the US inflation rate as measured by the Consumer Price Index (CPI) are plotted against the US unemployment rate for the period since 1960. It is hard to discern any systematic relationship in these data; indeed it is possible to argue that, if there is any relationship between the two variables, it is positive, not negative.

The third contributing factor was a challenge to the theoretical foundations of the Phillips curve analysis. In the late 1960s Milton Friedman (1968) and

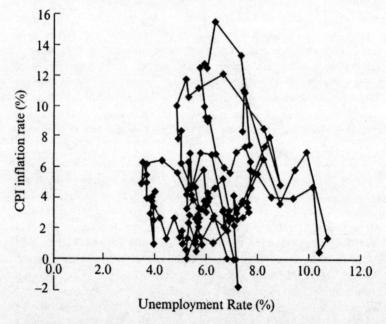

Figure 7.1   Inflation – unemployment trade-off

Edmund Phelps (1967) argued that the existing attempts to provide a theoretical foundation for a macroeconomic inflation–unemployment trade-off were flawed because they failed to distinguish between real and nominal variables. These authors argued that any theoretical Phillips curve should be 'shifty', and that the principal source of the shifts in the inflation–unemployment relationship was not any of the many variables that had been introduced with various empirical analyses, but rather was the revision of expectations about future inflation in response to new information. This represents the birth of the 'expectations augmented Phillips curve' which identifies two principal sources of inflation: the expectation of the present inflation rate that is inherited from the past and deviations of unemployment (or real output) from 'natural unemployment' or 'natural output'. These latter concepts represented the rate of unemployment or the level of output that can be expected to prevail in an environment where there are no surprises about the rate of inflation and all the labour and capital resources in the economy are utilized at sustainable rates.

Friedman and Phelps combined their theory of the 'expectations augmented Phillips curve' with an adaptive theory for the formation of inflation expectations (the expected rate of inflation depends on the observed history of the inflation rate), to produce a macroeconomic model that had radically different implications for the response of real output to nominal money shocks. Their theory suggested the patterns of real output and inflation responses found in the Andersen–Carlson model estimates. Output responded positively to a nominal money stimulus in the short run, but over some longer-run horizon the real output response was extinguished and an inflation response was all that remained. A further implication of the Friedman/Phelps model was that the monetary authorities could sustain a change in real output only at the expense of ever-*accelerating* inflation. This became known as the accelerationist hypothesis.

The Friedman/Phelps theory of a transitory response of real output to a sustained monetary shock, but a permanent inflation response to maintained changes in money growth rates, was rapidly incorporated into empirical macroeconomic models by replacing 'Phillips curve structures' with 'expectations augmented Phillips curve' structures and adaptive expectations formation mechanisms. Numerous simulation analyses of the time pattern of real output and inflation responses to monetary shocks were conducted with US macroeconometric models. A frequent conclusion of these analyses was that the real output response built up to a peak after one or two years and then dissipated over a considerable horizon. In contrast, the inflation response initially was quite small (the short-run Phillips curve was quite flat) and approached its long-run levels only after a period of several years. Armed with these outputs, many analysts argued that attempts at disinflation through austere monetary policies would be very costly in terms of a substantial period of high unemployment and reduced real output growth. In their opinion an attempt to return to price stability from the rates of inflation observed in the late 1960s and early 1970s was not worth the cost.

Less than a decade elapsed before the Friedman/Phelps revolution was itself challenged. Lucas and Sargent, armed with the concept of rational expectations, argued that any systematic attempt at monetary manipulation that was correctly perceived in advance by economic agents would have no effect on real output. Their view was that agents would correctly perceive the inflationary consequences of such predictable monetary policies and incorporate these predictions into their expectations of future inflation. Hence, when the predictable changes in money were implemented, changes in inflationary expectations would cause the 'expectations augmented Phillips curve' to shift up or down simultaneously, so that the actual rate of inflation realized in the economy would be consistent with the predicted or expected rate of inflation. Under these conditions real output would remain at its natural rate and both the immediate and longer-run responses of real output to predictable monetary shocks would be zero. Surprise changes in the nominal money supply, either purely random behaviour on the part of the monetary authorities or the result of unannounced changes in the systematic implementation of monetary policy, would produce transitory deviations of real output from natural output, but such deviations would exist only in the presence of inflation-forecasting errors. Under the rational expectations hypothesis such forecast errors could only be short-lived. Conversely, predictable monetary actions would be principally observed in changes in prices and inflation. The time pattern of the price level and inflation responses here depends on how fast velocity responds to the changes in nominal interest rates as a result of the adjustment of inflation expectations.

The initial interpretation of this newly advanced theory was the impression that the absence of any response of real output to predictable nominal monetary shocks and the absence of any persistence of real output responses to nominal money surprises was a characteristic of all models that featured rational expectations and an aggregate supply curve that made inflation only a function of inflation expectations and deviations of output from 'natural output'. This notion was contradicted by the research of Fischer (1979) and Taylor (1980) who showed that three conditions were required to produced the responses implied by the Lucas/Sargent type models. Not only did the models require rational expectations and a 'natural rate hypothesis', but they also required that nominal wages and prices adjust to market clearing conditions within the time period under consideration. Fischer and Taylor introduced multi-period overlapping nominal wage contracts into the rational expectations–natural rate models and showed that in these structures both predictable and surprise monetary actions generated persistent effects upon real output, though the size of the real output response to the two types of shocks differed. Though persistent, these responses are not permanent, and in the long run (steady-state equilibrium) in such models the real output response to either type of shock is zero. In effect the nominal wage inertia inherent in the Fischer/Taylor-type models reconstructs the implications of the Friedman/Phelps models in a rational expectations environment. The source of the short-run real output effects in these models is an information asymmetry between private agents and the policy authorities. Private agents commit to nominal wage contracts for an extended period of time based on a particular information set. Subsequently, during the period when the contract determining nominal wages is fixed, the policy authorities can reveal actions that were not previously predictable, and the nominal wages cannot adjust to the market equilibrium under this new information for the duration of the outstanding contracts. The assumption of overlapping wage contract periods generates the persistent real output response: in effect, as time passes, the fraction of nominal wages that are held invariant to the new information gradually declines until, when all nominal wage contracts have incorporated the information of the revealed monetary shock, the real output response is eliminated.

The Fischer/Taylor research has produced three distinctly different reactions and research agendas. The fundamental criticism levelled against these type of models is that the existence of the wage contract structure has no economic foundation. No rationale is provided whereby maximizing agents would find it in their interest to enter such contractual arrangements. One response is to pursue a research agenda to develop models that mimic observed 'stylized facts' of macroeconomic observations from structures that assume nominal wage and price flexibility. This, broadly speaking, is the agenda of the 'Real Business Cycle' or 'New Classical' approach to macroeconomics. A second response is to augment traditional microecomomic utility and profit-maximizing structures with various adjustment cost features that produce markets with 'sticky wage and/or price' behaviour. This is the agenda of the 'New Keynesian' approach to macroeconomics. A third approach is to acknowledge wage and price stickiness as the reality of many markets in advanced economies over long periods of history. This view accepts the origin of such pricing practices in information and/or transactions costs that are not modelled, and focuses attention, not on the existence of transitory real output responses to monetary shocks, nor on the microfoundations for the existence of such effects, but on measurement of the magnitude and duration of such responses.

A common characteristic of all of these approaches is that any response of real output to monetary shocks is a component of the transitory or cyclical variation in real output. In terms of the 'expectations augmented Phillips curve' paradigm, real output fluctuations induced by monetary forces are part of the fluctuation of real output around 'natural output'. Thus, if the transitory fluctuations in real output can be separated from permanent fluctuations, an upper bound can be determined for the effect of monetary shocks.

Money, prices and the real economy

It is always dangerous to attribute a fundamental influence on the views of macroeconomists to any empirical study, since the overwhelming majority of inferences from empirical macroeconomics have not been supported outside the sample period of the analysis. One empirical analysis that has important implications for the question of how nominal money shocks influence real output, and has withstood the onslaught of new data, is that of Nelson and Plosser (1982) Their analysis of a wide range of US macroeconomic time series found that many, if not most series, can be characterized as 'difference stationary' processes. Stripping this conclusion of the jargon, the implication of the analysis is that the principal force(s) generating the observations are permanent rather than transitory shocks. In particular, they argue that the dominant forces generating the observed behaviour of real output measures are such permanent shocks. Other analyses have replicated this conclusion with data from other countries or with more recent data from the US economy.

This characterization of the sources of real output fluctuations is not supportive of a major influence of nominal money shocks on real output. In macroeconomic structures which contain an expectations augmented Phillips curve, the influence of monetary shocks on real output results from inflation expectation errors. Such errors are transitory. In models with wage and price stickiness the effects of monetary shocks on real output can be persistent but are transitory. If the major source of variation in real output is generated by permanent shocks, then in conventional theoretical macroeconomic models such fluctuations cannot be of monetary origin. Variation in real output that is primarily generated by permanent shocks is more consistent with real business cycle theories that emphasize technology-based output fluctuations and with a conclusion that monetary shocks have not been the dominant source of economic fluctuations, at least over the past 50 years.

There are at least two reasons for taking a cautious approach to dismissing any role for monetary shocks in generating real output fluctuations based on evidence for permanent shocks to real output. First, it is very difficult to discriminate an economic time series generated as the result of truly permanent shocks from a time series that is generated by transitory but extremely persistent shocks. Christiano and Eichenbaum (1990) entitled their careful analysis of this issue 'Unit Roots in GNP: Do We Know, and Do We Care?' They conclude that it is probably impossible to know whether GNP has a component that is generated by permanent shocks, and that possibly it is not too important to be able to make a precise determination, since the presence or absence of a permanent shock component may not be a decisive factor in determining the role of monetary and fiscal policies as a source of economic fluctuations.

Second, in the early 1980s the Vector Autoregression Model (VAR) emerged as a popular tool with which to conduct empirical investigations of the impact of monetary shocks on real output and inflation (see Appendix of this chapter for brief description of this model). The initial investigations focused on small models involving a monetary aggregate such as M1 or the monetary base, real output and inflation. The results of such investigations appeared to support an effect of monetary shocks on real output such as that implied by Andersen–Jordan-type single equation analyses. Subsequent analyses broadened the scope of the investigation to include nominal interest rates. The typical conclusion from these expanded studies was that, once the impact of interest rate shocks had been considered, there was very little effect of shocks to monetary aggregates on real output. Cagan (1989) reviewed a large number of such studies covering many countries and dismissed this line of research because 'the VAR seems to me to be hopelessly unreliable and low in power to detect monetary effects of the kind we are looking for and believe, from other kinds of evidence, to exist' (ibid., p. 127).

There are at least two significant reasons to be sceptical of the claims made in many of the early VAR analyses of the effect of monetary shocks. First, many of these analyses were constructed in a mechanical fashion, with relatively little attention to the implied economic structure of the economic system. In order to determine the responses of the observed variables of the VAR system to the unobservable concepts such as interest rate shocks or monetary shocks, researchers applied arbitrary transformations to the estimated residuals of the VAR regression equations. In retrospect it appears that they did not always recognize that such transformations represented implicit assumptions about the underlying economic structure. The implicit economic structure is rarely discussed in these studies and frequently it did not characterize the form of any established theory of the role of money in the macroeconomy. In these cases, it is not clear that the failure to find any effect on real output from the constructed monetary shocks has any implication for the role of monetary policy in the economy. The results may just reflect a badly constructed set of supplementary assumptions that fail to define the monetary shocks that have affected the economy in the past.

A second problem with early VAR studies is the failure to represent an economy that is subject to both permanent and transitory shocks. These VAR studies either modelled levels of various macroeconomic time series, in which case they ignored the results of the Nelson/Plosser analysis and similar studies that suggested most such variables contain a component generated by permanent shocks, or they modelled first differences of the time series, in which case all shocks driving the macroeconomy are assumed to be permanent. The latter specification contradicts the accepted theory that the effect of nominal money shocks on real output has no permanent consequences. Hence the differenced models are incapable of detecting monetary responses consistent with any of the competing theories.

More recently, an alternative line of recent empirical research has focused on viewing economic time series, including real GDP, as mixtures of both permanent and transitory shocks in the context of VARs. These extended VAR models, known as Vector Error Correction Models, can accommodate an economic structure that is subject to such diverse forces as technology shocks which produce permanent real output responses but transitory inflation responses as well as monetary shocks which produce transitory real output responses but permanent inflation responses. An early example of this approach is that of King *et al.*, (1991). The approach in such studies is, as in the earlier VAR analyses, to decompose the forecast errors at various future horizons into fractions originating with different shocks. A typical result from such studies is that, at 'business cycle horizons', for example, forecasts two to four years into the future, permanent shocks are shown to account for almost all of the variance in forecast errors. At shorter forecasting horizons, such as zero to two years, a substantial fraction of the variance in forecast errors of real GDP is associated with transitory shocks. Such results appear to leave open the possibility of a substantial influence of nominal money shocks on real output for a reasonable, though not prolonged, period of time.

While such empirical findings leave open the possibility of a persistent effect of nominal shocks on real output, they do not prove the case. There are many possible sources of transitory shocks that can affect any economy. Separating the effects of monetary shocks from the effects of all other possible transitory shocks is no small undertaking. Such a determination cannot be made from observed data alone. It requires prior assumptions derived from a specification (economic model) of how the economy works. Econometricians refer to such prior assumptions as identifying restrictions. As we have discussed above, most macroeconomists accept characterization of the long-run behaviour of the macroeconomy, but there is considerable disagreement over the appropriate model of dynamics of a macroeconomy. Such disputes translate into a lack of usable identifying restrictions for the applied researcher. Each conjecture about macroeconomic dynamics translates into a different set of identifying restrictions, which in principle when applied to a given data set imply different responses of the economy to monetary shocks. Thus the influence of monetary policy on real output cannot be settled by pure data analysis. Ultimately the answer to the question, 'Can we know how monetary policy affects real output in the short run?' requires the development of theoretical models which provide more precisely defined testable propositions about the dynamic structure of the aggregate economy.

VAR and vector error correction models represent a distinct break with the previous generation of 'large structural econometric models' that characterized academic applied macroeconomic research in the 1960s and early 1970s. The popularity of the latter diminished after the 'rational expectations revolution' in macroeconomics which demonstrated that the implementation of this modelling strategy in the 1960s and early 1970s had the potential to generate inappropriate inferences if economic agents formed expectations in a forward-looking fashion. The 'structural econometric' modelling approach has been revived in a form that incorporates forward-looking expectations. The pioneer in this type of analysis is John Taylor (1993), who has constructed single- and multi-country macroeconomic models incorporating the rational expectations hypothesis and sticky nominal wages. Since the structure of these empirical models conforms to that of the Fischer/Taylor-type theoretical models, it necessarily implies that nominal money shocks produce transitory real output responses. The only issue to investigate is the size and duration of such responses.

In summary, sharp divisions of professional opinion prevail regarding the short-run impact of nominal monetary shocks on the macroeconomy. While the resolution of this dispute is fundamentally an empirical problem, success in narrowing the range of possible outcomes requires not only better empirical analyses, but also progress in developing theoretical models which define more precisely the dynamics implicit in the competing hypotheses. Without the guidance of such theoretical restrictions, arbitrary supplementary restrictions can be applied to any data analysis to produce a wide range of alternative quantitative implications about the influence of money on real output.

BIBLIOGRAPHY

Andersen L.C. and K.M. Carlson (1970), 'A Monetarist Model for Economic Stabilization', *Federal Reserve Bank of St Louis Review*, **52** (April), 7–21.

Andersen, L.C. and J.L. Jordan (1968), 'Monetary and Fiscal Actions: A Test of Their Relative Importance in Stabilization Policies', *Federal Reserve Bank of St Louis Review*, **50** (November), 11–24.

Cagan, P. (1989), 'Money-Income Causality – A Critical Review of the Literature Since *A Monetary History*', in M.D. Bordo (ed.), *Money, History and International Finance: Essays in Honor of Anna J. Schwartz*, The University of Chicago Press, pp.-117–51.

Christiano, L.J. and M. Eichenbaum (1990), 'Unit Roots in GNP: Do We Know and Do We Care?', *Carnegie-Rochester Conference Series on Public Policy*, **32** (Spring), 7–52.

Fischer S. (1979), 'Long-term Contracting, Sticky Prices and Monetary Policy', *Journal of Political Economy*, **85**, 191–206.

Friedman, M. (1968), 'The Role of Monetary Policy', *American Economic Review*, **58**,-1–17.

Friedman, M. and A.J. Schwartz (1963), *A Monetary History of the United States 1867–1960*, Princeton: Princeton University Press.

King, R.G., C.I. Plosser, J.H. Stock and M.W. Watson (1991), 'Stochastic Trends and Economic Fluctuations', *American Economic Review*, **81**, 819–40.

Nelson, C.R. and C.I. Plosser (1982), 'Trends and Random Walks in Macroeconomic Time Series: Some Evidence and Implications', *Journal of Monetary Economics*, **10**,-139–62.
Phelps, E.S. (1967), 'Phillips Curves, Expectations of Inflation and Optimal Unemployment over Time', *Economica*, **34**, 254–81.
Phillips, A.W. (1958), 'The Relation between Unemployment and the Rate of Change of Money Wages in the U.K. 1862–1957'. *Economica*, **25**, 283–99.
Taylor, J.B. (1980), 'Aggregate Dynamics and Staggered Contracts', *Journal of Political Economy*, **86**, 1–23.
Taylor, J.B. (1993), *Macroeconomic Policy in a World Economy*, W.W. Norton.

VECTOR AUTOREGRESSION MODELS (VARS)

An empirical vector autoregression is a set of estimated equations in which each variable in the model is regressed on lagged values of itself and lagged values of all the other variables in the model. For example, a two-variable, first-order VAR in variables X_1 and X_2 would be specified as:

$$X_{1t} = a_0 + a_1 X_{1t-1} + a_2 X_{2t-1} + e_{1t} \tag{7.1}$$
$$X_{2t} = b_0 + b_1 X_{1t-1} + b_2 X_{2t-1} + e_{2t} \tag{7.2}$$

where the a_i and b_i are estimated regression coefficients and the e_i are the disturbance terms or residuals of the equations. VARs are generalized to higher order systems by adding additional lags on each variable in each equation, and to higher dimension by adding additional variables and additional equations.

Now it is well recognized that VARs fall into the class of models known in the econometric literature as 'reduced form models', and that the disturbance terms indicated by the e_is in general are linear combinations of all the 'economic' shocks that influence the variables indicated by the Xs. The analyst wishing to determine how a policy action (such as either an unexpected change in a monetary or fiscal policy variable or a change in the rule by which the central bank conducts monetary policy) affects the economy must extract a measure of the historical values of the 'monetary' or 'fiscal' policy shocks from the reduced form residuals, e_{it}. This extraction process, known in the econometrics literature as 'identification', involves imposing a set of restrictions on the data series. Ideally such restrictions are derived from a theoretical framework that specifies how variables in the macroeconomy are interrelated. Alternatively arbitrary sets of restrictions can be imposed upon the data. If the restrictions imposed to extract the measures of the 'economic shocks' include restrictions that such shocks are uncorrelated, then so-called 'impulse response analyses' can be constructed which trace the way in which the effect of any of the constructed 'economic' shocks is transmitted over time through the economy.

8. Designing the post-modern bank safety net: lessons from developed and developing economies

Charles W. Calomiris

INTRODUCTION

This chapter reviews the changes that have taken place over the twentieth century in policies and attitudes regarding the government 'safety net' for the financial system. It begins by reviewing the period of expansion of protection from the 1930s to the early 1980s, which saw the construction of an extensive 'modern' safety net, and then discusses how new evidence began to alter attitudes and policies in the mid-1980s, in the USA and in other economies. Next alternative solutions to the incentive problems of the safety net are considered, with a comparison of the Basle approach and a potentially more promising approach to reforming government safety nets – one that relies on market discipline via a subordinated debt financing requirement. Finally, the chapter reviews and evaluates two prominent examples of recent reform in the light of earlier arguments – namely the experiences of Chile and Argentina, which have injected elements of private market discipline into their safety net reforms – and a brief summary concludes.

THE EVOLUTION OF THE MODERN FINANCIAL SAFETY NET

Prior to 1933, throughout the world the government's direct role as an insurer of financial stability was relatively modest. Indirectly – via monetary, fiscal and debt-management policies – government actions sometimes contributed to stability or instability. Historically governments also licensed (and in some cases owned significant stakes in) private financial institutions. But microeconomic government interventions – subsidized lending, insurance of private institutions' claims or government recapitalization of particular institutions – were relatively uncommon.

In the USA, at first the Federal Reserve (Fed) loaned reserves to banks only against high-quality collateral assets, a practice that rendered the Fed helpless in preventing the failures of banks whose depositors had lost faith in their solvency, since riskless lending (even at a subsidized rate) is of very limited value to a troubled institution financed by short-term (demandable) debt. This was not perceived as a deficiency by the Fed's founders, who saw it primarily as a vehicle for smoothing fluctuations in the seasonal supply of reserves and, consequently, seasonal movements in the riskless money market interest rate. To the extent that the Fed was to act as a lender of last resort during crises, its role was to expand the aggregate supply of reserves, not to provide subsidized lending against questionable collateral or to try to rescue banks. The Fed was not willing to lend to banks in a way that placed it in a junior position relative to banks' depositors. By being unwilling to accept risky bank loans of uncertain value as collateral, the Fed ensured that, if depositors lost faith in the (unobservable) value of a bank's loan portfolio, that bank would fail.

In Britain, Bagehot's maxim for the lender of last resort – to lend freely at a penalty rate during a crisis – had inspired some limited government intervention during financial crises that went beyond Fed discount lending policy. For example, the Bank of England's line of credit to the bank syndicate that bailed out Barings in 1890 placed the Bank of England in a junior risk position relative to the depositors of the London banks. Such assistance was capable of better averting bank failures, since the lender of last resort was willing to take on default risk in a way that mitigated the incentives of depositors to withdraw funds from banks during uncertain times. It is worth emphasizing, however, that the assistance by the Bank of England placed it at minimal risk, and *maximized the privatization of risk* during the crisis of 1890. The arrangement between the banks and the Bank of England placed the latter in a senior position relative to the individual stockholders of the London banks, who were jointly liable for losses from the Barings bail-out.

In many countries, especially since the nineteenth century, banks and governments had also acted as partners in special ways during wartime. Governments sometimes relied on banks to assist in war finance in exchange for protection of the banks from failure if the value of government debt fell. And in some cases – for example, the protection afforded US banks during the Civil War (Calomiris, 1991) – government used its power to define the numeraire in the economy (and to suspend convertibility of that numeraire into hard currency) to protect banks from adverse changes in the government financial position.

Notwithstanding all these interventions, by modern (mid-to-late twentieth-century) standards pre-1930s governments were sceptical of the merits of publicly managed and publicly funded assistance to financial institutions during peacetime. There is clear evidence that government stinginess was not the result of any ignorance of economic externalities associated with bank failures, but rather reflected appreciation of the moral hazard consequences of providing bailouts (Calomiris, 1989, 1990, 1992, 1993a; Flood, 1992). The primary sources of protection against the risk of depositor runs on a bank were other banks. That assistance was not guaranteed, but rather depended on the willingness of private coalitions of bankers to provide protection to a threatened institution (Gorton, 1985; Calomiris, 1989, 1990; 1993b; Calomiris and Gorton, 1991; Calomiris and Schweikart, 1991; Calomiris and Mason, 1997).

Attitudes changed in the 1930s. In the USA, in 1932, President Hoover gave in to pressure to provide a new source of government lending to banks and other firms in distress – the Reconstruction Finance Corporation (RFC). Initially, the RFC, like the Fed, was authorized only to lend against high-quality collateral. In 1933, however, its authority was extended to permit the purchase of the preferred stock of banks. That change was important. RFC lending on high-quality collateral provided no subsidy to distressed institutions and econometric analysis of the impact of such lending suggests that it did not prevent banks from failing. In contrast, preferred stock purchases did reduce the probability of failure for distressed institutions (Mason, 1996). Collateral and eligibility requirements on Fed discount window lending were also relaxed in the wake of the Depression (Schwartz, 1992; Calomiris and Wheelock, 1998).

Additionally federal deposit insurance – a concept that, prior to 1933, was viewed as a transparent attempt to subsidize small, high-risk banks – passed in 1933 as part of a complex political compromise between the House and Senate banking committees (Calomiris and White, 1994). New programmes to provide price supports for farmers, and subsidized credit for mortgages, farms, small businesses and other purposes followed, often justified by arguments that they would 'stabilize' credit markets and limit unwarranted financial distress.

Thus began the 'modern age' of government intervention to 'stabilize' the financial system. By the 1950s and 1960s, many of the Depression era reforms had achieved the status of unquestionable wisdom. They constituted part of the new 'automatic stabilizers' lauded by macroeconomists as insurance against a financial collapse like that of the 1930s. In retrospect, we now know that the 1950s and 1960s were an unusually stable period characterized by low commodity and asset price volatility. But many economists at the time attributed the economic stability of that period to the new 'stabilizing' government safety net.

In the immediate post-World War II environment many countries followed the lead of the USA in establishing aggressive financial 'safety nets'. The new Bretton Woods institutions – the World Bank and the International Monetary Fund – were also conceived in the heady atmosphere of the late 1940s. Confidence was widespread that financial assistance from governments, or coalitions of governments, to absorb private default risk would pave the way for worldwide economic growth and stability.

The new financial safety net constructed in the 1930s remained essentially untested during the first 40 years of its existence. The volatile environment of the 1970s and 1980s provided the first test. The shocks to asset prices, exchange rates and commodity prices of the 1970s and 1980s reminded economists that volatility has always been the norm. More importantly, it disabused them of their optimism about the stabilizing effects of the financial safety net by demonstrating how drastically different the behaviour of protected banks (and their regulators) could be once adverse shocks significantly weakened the capital position of banks. The possibility that, under adverse circumstances, banks would consciously abuse the safety net, or that regulators and supervisors would consciously avoid their duty, seemed remote in the 1960s. As we shall see, the experience of the 1970s and 1980s changed those perceptions.

The 1970s undermined the confidence in macroeconomic 'fine tuning' that had reigned in the 1960s, but it was the 1980s and 1990s that saw a worldwide transformation in thinking about the stabilizing effects of the financial safety net. Initially the bank failures in the USA seemed to be the result of exogenous influences: monetary policy and shocks to commodity prices. The rise in interest rates had put much of the savings and loan industry into insolvency by 1982 (Barth and Bartholomew, 1992). The combination of high oil prices, high interest rates and the decline in dollar prices of commodities sent US agriculture into a tailspin in the early 1980s. Related shocks to developing countries that were heavy borrowers, like Brazil, brought new challenges for sovereign borrowers and their banks. The 1982 collapse of oil prices sent new shock waves through oil-producing areas such as Mexico, Texas, Oklahoma and Venezuela, and the banks that had financed the oil exploration boom of the 1970s. Chile's financial system faced unprecedented strain as the price of copper fell, and later as the US interest rate rises of the early 1980s pulled foreign capital out of Chile, and set the stage for the collapse of its fixed exchange rate.

Initially the financial distress of the early 1980s was perceived as reinforcing the argument for an aggressive safety net. The farm debt crisis that gripped US farmers in the early 1980s brought calls for more subsidies, more lending and debt moratoria. Distressed savings and loans (S&Ls) cried out for regulatory relief, and in 1982 were given new powers to raise insured funds and to invest them in highly risky assets. They were also granted a new form of accounting (Regulatory Accounting Principles) to avoid recognizing losses to capital when asset values fell. The collapse of less developed country (LDC) debt also brought calls for moratoria, and for assistance from international agencies.

The first major American financial institution made insolvent through its exposure to oil price risk – Penn Square – was allowed to fail in 1982. But the US government changed that policy in 1983, when Continental Illinois was faced with a 'silent run' on its uninsured debt. The government concluded that Continental was 'too big to fail', and decided to recapitalize the bank, thus protecting not only insured depositors, but uninsured claimants on the bank as-well.

The Fed also participated to an unprecedented degree in discount window lending to insolvent financial institutions during the mid-1980s. That lending did not place the Fed at significant risk (since its special legal status gives it a senior, collateralized claim on bank assets), but it did allow insolvent institutions to continue to lend and meet their reserve requirements, and the government insurers of banks bore the burden of the continuing losses from permitting these so-called 'zombies' to remain active. The Fed did so with the wholehearted approval of the Federal Deposit Insurance Corporation (FDIC), which hoped to postpone the realization of losses as long as possible, given the low level of its funds. The anticipated political costs of publicizing these losses (especially prior to the election of 1988) gave elected officials the incentive to encourage such 'regulatory forbearance' on the part of the agencies that insured the losses of financial institutions (Kane, 1989, 1992).

The pendulum of political support for such broad protection began to swing back in the mid-1980s. It became increasingly clear that financial risk was not all exogenous – much of it had been chosen by institutions and individuals that knew they were protected (at taxpayers' expense) from downside loss. The notion that risk was being subsidized by the government, and consequently being purposefully increased by financial institutions, was viewed as late as the early 1980s as the unrealistic hypothesis of a handful of financial economists. In a matter of several years, however, amidst mounting evidence of purposeful risk taking by banks with impunity, the minority critique became the consensus view, both in the USA and abroad.

Thus the safety net, previously lauded as a risk reducer, came to be viewed by many as the single most important destabilizing influence in the financial system. It is interesting to review how that transformation in thinking came about and how it led to a new post-modern movement to reform the safety net.

QUESTIONING THE SAFETY OF THE SAFETY NET

The savings and loan crisis in the USA was of central importance in galvanizing the debate over safety net reform. It provided clear, sometimes sensational, evidence of ways in which government protection of financial institutions could be abused. The evidence that much of the loss experienced within the industry was the result of legal, voluntary risk taking and fraud (rather than exogenous shocks) had a particularly striking effect on the academic debate.

Barth and Bartholomew (1992) provided descriptive evidence of the mismanagement of the savings and loans that created the largest costs to taxpayers. Many of those losses were produced *after* these institutions had become insolvent. With little or no capital at stake, these institutions used the new powers granted them in 1982 to increase their asset risk and to grow at a phenomenal rate, financed by insured deposits. This costly strategy made sense from the standpoint of an insolvent S&L. Only a combination of rapid growth and high profits would restore the capital of the institution, providing it with a new lease on life.

Horvitz (1992) drew attention to this 'moral hazard' problem in his analysis of the behaviour of Texas banks and thrifts. He argued that losses of capital led these institutions to increase their asset risk (the opposite of prudent bank practice) because their low capital levels implied little risk of further loss and significant upside gains to bank stockholders. Texas institutions that experienced losses on oil exploration lending moved into the riskier business of financing commercial real estate development – an even riskier version of their earlier failed 'bet' on oil exploration. Texas banks and thrifts suffered some of their worst losses as the result of this second round of risk taking, *after* the exogenous decline in oil prices and bank capital had occurred.

Brewer (1995) provided formal evidence consistent with the arguments of Barth and Bartholomew, Horvitz and others. He showed that capital losses had encouraged asset reallocation towards higher risk. More importantly he showed that, for low-capital institutions, the decision to increase asset risk resulted in an increase in the market value of the institution's stock. In other words, not only were institutions taking advantage of the subsidization of risk offered by deposit insurance, but doing so created value for stockholders and was perceived as doing so in the stock market.

The evidence on abuse of the safety net by savings and loans served the important function of providing legitimacy to economic arguments about perverse incentives from deposit insurance. It was no longer possible to argue that concerns about incentives were unrealistic, that bankers were simply the victims of exogenous shocks or that bankers were not the sort of people who would willingly assume imprudent risk just to increase expected profit.

Nor were savings and loan failures and the oil-related bank collapse in Texas and Oklahoma the only examples of moral hazard costs from government risk subsidization. Carey (1990) analysed the boom and bust in US agricultural land and commodity prices and lending during the 1970s and 1980s, and its relationship to government policies to provide 'liquidity' to farmers. One of the legacies of the Great Depression was the Farm Credit System, a network of government-guaranteed financial institutions that specialize in mortgage and working capital lending to farmers. Somewhat like a lender of last resort, the Farm Credit System has government protection and a mandate to maintain credit supply to farmers. It also displays less demanding collateral standards for lending. Carey found a close relationship between government-sponsored credit (via the Farm Credit System) and excessive risk taking by farmers. The Farm Credit System was increasingly willing to lend against questionable collateral (land) during the boom, while private banks withdrew from the market as lending risk increased.

Interestingly, early twentieth-century American financial history provides additional evidence of the moral hazard costs of deposit insurance, and the potential for insured (subsidized) bank lending to drive speculative booms in agricultural real estate. Calomiris (1989, 1990, 1993a) argued that state-level deposit insurance schemes in several states during and after World War I promoted unwarranted agricultural expansion during the war, and extreme loss in the face of postwar declines in commodity and land prices.

As all this new evidence of moral hazard in banking mounted in the late 1980s, financial economists familiar with the savings and loan, oil lending and agricultural lending crises considered other areas of potential weakness in the incentive structure of the American financial system. The two most important potential areas of weakness were large commercial centre banks (covered by implicit 'too-big-to-fail' insurance) and life insurance companies (covered by state-level insurance schemes). Many of these institutions had experienced large losses in their commercial real estate portfolios, some of which followed tax law changes in 1986 that limited accelerated depreciation for commercial real estate transactions.

Some evidence suggests that life insurers and large banks that had experienced significant capital losses were shifting into high-risk assets under the cover of explicit or implicit insurance protection. Brewer and Mondschean (1993) and Brewer *et al.* (1992) found evidence of moral hazard in the portfolio choices of life insurance companies that is reminiscent of Brewer's (1995) evidence for savings and loans. Boyd and Gertler (1994) found that the largest US banks had loan loss rates on commercial loans five times those of small banks, and loss rates on construction loans nearly 10 times those of small banks (as of 1992). They argued that regional factors did not explain those differences and concluded that part, if not all, of the higher risk of large banks reflected the incentive to take risks offered by the 'too-big-to-fail' doctrine.

While there was never a collapse of US money centre banks or life insurers, one could argue that the collapse was only narrowly averted by the rebound in the economy after 1991. Several consecutive years of profits have now recapitalized these institutions, reduced their probabilities of failure and thereby lessened their incentives to assume excessive risk. But in 1990 and 1991 some commentators claimed that some US money centre banks were insolvent or near insolvent, and that others were barely solvent and unable to borrow extensively on the federal funds market. If the recession had persisted into 1992 or 1993, it is conceivable that large US banks and life insurance companies might have continued to increase their portfolio risk, experienced losses and eventually been granted a massive bail-out from federal and state governments.

Thus far, we have focused on the US experience, but the US was neither the first nor the worst case of financial collapse during the 1980s and 1990s. The Chilean experience was arguably the first clear case of the two-stage pattern discussed above. A decline in copper prices, and other exogenous shocks that worsened Chile's position internationally, were followed by regulatory forbearance and government assumption of the risks in the banking system. This promoted new risk taking by banks and their borrowers and culminated in the costly collapse of many financial institutions. One of the primary risks that engaged subsidized speculation was the risk of currency devaluation, which banks and their borrowers bet against heavily in 1981 and 1982. When devaluation came, the (government-assumed) losses were enormous.

As in many other countries, the adverse macroeconomic consequences of the initial exogenous shocks to the Chilean economy made it politically difficult to impose the necessary discipline on banks. As de la Cuadra (then Minister of Finance) and Valdes (1992, p. 75) argue, 'In a nutshell, we argue that the superintendency could not include in its loan classification procedure a truly independent assessment of the exposure of bank debtors to foreign exchange and interest rate risk because such an assessment would have interfered with official macroeconomic policies.' De la Cuadra and Valdes go on to trace how excess risk taking by banks and firms, and eventual losses from those risks, produced economic devastation by 1982 and increasingly perverse incentives for lenders (ibid., pp. 79–80). Their discussion warrants recounting in detail.

In 1981 most banks saw their effective capital plummet further as soon as optimistic debtors became less willing to pay when the net worth of their corporations fell. This reluctance reinforced the previous perverse incentives to banks, so that banks became even more willing to assume credit risks derived from exchange rate and interest rate-risks.

By 1981 financing decisions by Chilean firms and banks reflected a *de facto* government guarantee to the private sector for foreign exchange risk. Our analysis has identified the superintendency's lack of penalization of credit risk in its loan classification criteria as the channel for the guarantee.

The outcome of this structural contingent subsidy was that many small and medium-sized businesses got deeply into debt in 1981. Debts to banks increased during 1981 from 37.6 percent to 50.4 percent of GDP in response to the rise in real interest rates...

By mid-1982 the fall in GDP was so steep that it took on the character of a depression. In June 1982 the government finally decided to devalue the exchange rate by 14 percent...By the end of 1982 the losses that the devaluations had inflicted on the holders of dollar-denominated debts had created insolvency among firms of all-sizes....

The sorry state of most debtors caused delinquent loans to rise from 2.34 percent of loans in December 1981 to 3.83 percent in February 1982 and 6.31 percent in

May. Most delinquent loans turned out to be 100 percent losses, so they reduced the
net worth of banks…
…On July 12, 1982 the central bank decided to allow banks to defer their losses over
several years, so it began to buy the banks' delinquent loan portfolios at face value.
The banks, however, had to promise to repurchase the portfolios at face value over
time with 100 percent of their profits, so the scheme did not improve bank solvency by
itself. It solved a liquidity problem but also set the stage for making good the implicit
contingent subsidy that the government had offered to speculators in 1981.

The authors go on to emphasize that loans to industrial firms that were
linked to banks via conglomerates were especially forthcoming from banks as
a consequence of the government subsidization of risk. Thus, despite its free
market orientation and stated commitment to market discipline in banking, Chile
ended up insuring 'uninsured' claims on banks, subsidizing high-risk resurrection
strategies on the part of its banks and passing on enormous risk-encouraging
credit subsidies to large industrial firms with close links to banks.

The Chilean and US examples were followed by a wave of banking disasters
in other countries, against which the banking collapses of the 1930s pale by
comparison. Many of the cases bear a strong resemblance to the Chilean and
US examples. Recent surveys by Caprio and Klingebiel (1996a, 1996b) and
Lindgren *et al.* (1996) have demonstrated how widespread the problem of
moral hazard has become in the financial system, spanning the globe and
including developed and developing economies. The lessons they draw from
these experiences are uniform: well-intentioned government lenders of last
resort (or insurers of deposits) have promoted both large deadweight losses
(from inefficient investments and restructuring costs) and enormous fiscal
strains on governments. Crises also seem to have an important disruptive effect
on post-crisis growth and investment rates, probably through the destruction of
institutional and human capital in the banking system.

A common denominator of the Chilean, Venezuelan, Mexican and Japanese
crises – each of which carries a price tag in excess of 10 per cent of their
respective country's GDP – is the extent to which the banking disaster, and
the unwillingess of governments to allow banks to suffer the consequences of
their own losses, resulted from a close 'partnership' between large industrial
groups (which controlled the major banks) and the government. These bank-
affiliated groups can take on the status of semi-public institutions. They maintain
enormous influence over government policy and see government protection of
banks as a key dimension of their relationship with the government.

With the exception of Chile, these countries' banking crises were 'resolved'
without addressing the moral hazard problems that underlay them. In Venezuela,
despite a commitment not to bail out banks, banks were bailed out at enormous
cost when regulators faced political constraints to do so (de Krivoy, 1995).
Little has been done to avoid the repetition of a similar crisis in the future. In

Mexico, the large banks were privatized in 1991, auctioned at a very high price to the country's largest industrialists. Mexican banks expanded their lending and portfolio risk on a virtually non-existent capital base. By 1993, the banking system was viewed as unstable if not insolvent, and posed the threat of a large potential fiscal drain on the government. The banks' weak financial conditions, losses on derivative positions abroad and their knowledge of their own potential impact on the Mexican government's ability to maintain its exchange rate policy led the banks themselves to aggravate the run on the peso in 1994, when they chose to liquidate their highly speculative bets against devaluation (Garber, 1997). The similarities to the Chilean experience are uncanny.

Despite the clear moral hazard lessons from the Mexican crisis, the political interests of the US Treasury Department the Mexican government and its foreign lenders have been best served by misinterpreting the peso crisis as an unwarranted run, resulting from a 'liquidity' problem that was produced by the short maturity structure of government debt and self-fulfilling adverse expectations. The US-sponsored bail-out of the Mexicans, partly in consequence of the absolution that accompanied it, has done nothing to improve the root causes of the crisis, including the financial structure of the banking system. Some accounting reforms have taken place, some new foreign entry into banking has been allowed and some recognition of loan losses (paid for by the government) has begun. But virtually nothing has been done to limit the future abuse of government insurance, which insures virtually all liabilities in the Mexican financial system.

The Japanese banking system has hidden its losses behind a veil of regulatory forbearance, hoping that improvement in economic performance will pay for bank loan losses. An outright bail-out of the banking system would have been unpopular in Japan, so forbearance has been the option of least political resistance. Of course, that solution ignores the incentive that low-capital institutions face to take on new risks. Thus the costs of the bail-out may grow over time, even as economic conditions improve.

Unlike Venezuela, Mexico and Japan, Chile moved aggressively, as early as 1986, to recognize and resolve the underlying incentive problems that had produced its financial crisis (see the detailed discussion below). Other countries, including the USA, Argentina, El Salvador, New Zealand and Malaysia, also began to take seriously some of the lessons of moral hazard and regulatory forbearance that underlie the many recent examples of financial crises.

The period 1988–93 witnessed unprecedented actions internationally, and especially in the USA, to limit safety net protection of banks. The passage of the Basle international bank capital standards in 1988 – imposing crude, risk-based capital standards on insured institutions – was the first step, and it was followed in the USA by the banking legislation of 1989 (implementing the standards and adding new limits on the activities of insured institutions) and the Federal

Deposit Insurance Corporation Improvement Act (FDICIA) in 1991 (establishing guidelines for 'prompt corrective action' to enforce the new standards).

The 1991 law also codified a limited version of the 'too-big-to-fail doctrine', but its intent was to limit its application. Under the 1991 law, for insurance to be extended to 'uninsured' bank liabilities (beginning in 1995), the FDIC, the Secretary of the Treasury (in consultation with the President) and a supernumerary majority of the boards of the FDIC and the Federal Reserve must agree that not doing so 'would have serious adverse effects on economic conditions or financial stability'. Also, if uninsured deposits are covered under this provision, the insurance fund must be reimbursed through emergency special assessments. Because the nation's largest banks would end up paying a disproportionate cost of such a bail-out, advocates of FDICIA argued that the large banks could be relied upon to lobby successfully against the extension of insurance to uninsured deposits, unless the criterion for assistance was truly met. Finally, in 1993, new limits on discount window lending were put in place by the Fed, to limit Fed lending to distressed banks and to avoid a repetition of the Fed's complicity in regulatory forbearance during the 1980s.

Despite the progress that has been made in the USA, one can question whether these new and better government rules, implemented by government regulators and supervisors, are really a promising approach to resolving incentive problems attendant upon the financial safety net. Do government supervisors possess the skill and the incentive to identify capital losses in banks as diligently as would private market agents with their own money on the line? Will supervisors or regulators be tempted to ignore losses when it is politically expedient for them, or their superiors, to do so? Are existing measures of asset risk, or existing requirements for various types of capital, likely to result in prudent risk taking by banks, even if the new capital standards are enforced properly?

Clearly opportunities for increasing risk in ways not captured adequately by the Basle standards – particularly via exchange rate and interest rate derivatives – pose an important problem in this regard. It will also be argued below that an emphasis on equity capital, as opposed to subordinated debt capital, is an important weakness of the Basle approach. Doubts about the efficacy of the Basle–FDICIA approach to ensuring that the safety net is not abused have produced alternative approaches to managing safety net protection, to which we now turn.

THE POST-MODERN SAFETY NET

The Problem

The motivation for what we call the 'post-modern' safety net is to avoid abuse of government protection that arises when the cost banks pay for access to the safety net does not properly reflect their decisions to bear risk. Any meaningful reform of deposit insurance must either credibly restrict risk taking or make the cost of protection against losses to bank deposits sensitive to the riskiness of insured deposits. Doing either would remove any incentive for banks to increase risk in response to a capital loss, since they would receive no subsidy from raising their risk.

Figure 8.1 plots a deposit isorisk line for a 10 basis point default risk premium on bank deposits (as a point of reference), using the Black–Scholes option pricing formula to map from the combination of bank asset risk and bank leverage to the actuarily fair default (and insurance) premium on deposits (see Calomiris and Wilson, 1997, for further discussion of contingent claims models of bank liabilities). The intuition for Figure 8.1 is clear: the default risk on bank debt is a positive function of both asset risk and leverage. For a bank operating at point *A* (on the 10 basis point deposit isorisk line) the fair insurance premium on deposits (if all deposits are insured by the government) would be 10 basis points. Banks would pay the riskless rate of interest to depositors and 10 basis points to the government. If banks increased their asset risk (moving to point *B* in Figure 8.1), then the fair deposit insurance premium would rise to 20 basis points. So long as the government actually raises the insurance premium by 10

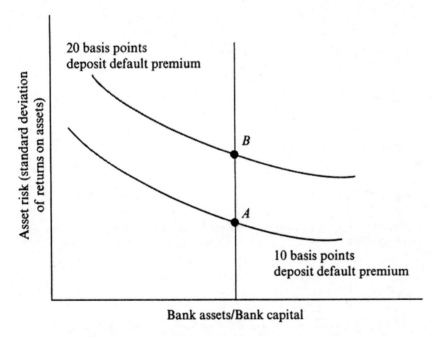

Figure 8.1   Deposit risk as a function of asset risk and leverage

basis points whenever banks move from *A* to *B*, banks will have no incentive to increase asset risk.

The problem is, however, that government supervisors and regulators may not behave ideally, either because they do not know the bank's true deposit default risk or because they face political incentives to ignore it. With respect to the first problem, recall that the unique characteristic of bank lending is the private information banks have about the value of their credit risks. Bank loans are costly for outsiders to value because doing so requires detailed understanding of the fundamental credit risks of firms that borrow from banks (many of which are not well known to outsiders), as well as an understanding of how to value the bank's claims on the firm, which typically entail a variety of idiosyncratic covenants and collateral provisions.

If banks can hide increases in deposit default risk, either by hiding loan losses or by disguising the riskiness of their portfolio, they can thereby avoid commensurate increases in insurance costs and obtain subsidies for increasing deposit risk. How do unregulated banking systems solve this 'agency' problem? How do uninsured depositors ensure that they are paid an adequate yield to compensate for the default risk they bear? Clearly the problem was not solved historically, and should not be solved today, by making banks' credit risks costlessly transparent. Doing so would require extreme restrictions on bank activities. The social value of banking arises from banks' specializing in information creation and contract enforcement (the so-called 'delegated monitoring' function of banks). Although this delegation makes it costly for outsiders to monitor the riskiness of bank assets, such intermediation is highly productive since it economizes on the costs of information and control by creating banks that specialize in these activities.

The historical solution to the agency problem is to be found in the contracting structure of banks and the incentives that structure creates in an unregulated banking system. Calomiris and Kahn (1991) and Calomiris *et al.* (1994) argue that banks operate as three-party arrangements bringing together 'insiders' (bank stockholder-managers), 'informed outsiders' (large depositors that specialize in monitoring bank activities) and 'uninformed depositors' (passive, small depositors). The uninformed relied on the informed depositors to monitor the banker. The 'first-come, first-served' rule for deposit withdrawals, along with a sufficient amount of bank reserves, provides pay-offs to informed monitors in 'bad' states of the world that induce them to invest in information about bank activities and to run the bank if they see a sufficiently bad state of the world. The threat of an informed run, or an actual informed run, obviate agency (moral hazard) costs that would otherwise arise from the fact that bankers have private information about the quality of their assets.

Because bank regulators and supervisors do not face strong incentives to invest in information (as would private depositors), it is less likely that they will be as well informed about the true risk characteristics of bank assets. Moreover political considerations may make regulators and supervisors unwilling to penalize banks for increasing their risk, even if the authorities can observe that an increase in risk or a decline in bank capital has taken place. This is particularly true during recession-induced bank 'capital crunches', when politicians and regulators face strong incentives to 'forbear' from strict enforcement of bank regulations in order to promote a larger supply of bank credit in the economy. The politically mandated forbearance of recent years – in the USA, Chile, Venezuela, Mexico, Japan and most recently in Korea, Indonesia and Thailand – provides little evidence that regulators can be relied upon to control politically powerful bankers, especially when governments face populist pressures to expand credit supply during a downturn.

In contrast, private, uninsured depositors can be counted upon to penalize banks for asset risk or leverage increases that produce higher default risk on deposits. Calomiris and Wilson (1997) find that New York City banks in the 1920s and 1930s faced strong pressure from depositors to limit default risk, and that this pressure contributed to banks' decisions to shed risky loans during the 1930s.[1] Those same pressures are visible today. Continental Illinois was effectively forced into the hands of the government in 1984 by a 'silent run' on the part of its uninsured depositors. Bank One faced the threat of similar problems temporarily in the mid-1990s, owing to the complexity of its derivatives positions and doubts by some of its creditors about the value and risk of those derivatives positions. To avoid market discipline, Bank One's executives met creditors privately for several days to explain their positions and reassure them, which they succeeded in doing.

The importance of asymmetric information (the lack of transparency of bank risk to outsiders) deserves emphasis. Absent asymmetric information (which makes it necessary for someone to invest credibly in monitoring bank risk and leverage) there would be no incentive problem in the safety net. The regulation of bank risk could be accomplished easily because deposit risk would be costlessly observable to everyone. But absent asymmetric information, there would also be no need for banks, much less a bank safety net. Ironically the very information problems that give rise to banks and to the desire for a safety net (to avoid banking panics) make it very difficult to ensure that the bank safety net will be incentive-compatible.[2]

Thus minimum capital requirements (which underlie the Basle standards and the recent American and Chilean reforms) offer an inadequate solution to safety net incentive problems. Capital standards fail to prevent the subsidization of risk, for two reasons. First, book capital standards constrain risk only so long as regulators and supervisors ensure that book capital bears a close relationship to true capital (that is, the implied market value of capital). But if bank losses are either not observed or not reported by supervisors, capital standards may have little force. Second, even if regulators enforce capital requirements by fully recognizing capital losses whenever they occur, capital standards alone do not obviate safety net subsidies for risk taking.

To see why this is so, consider the vertical line running through points *A* and *B* in Figure 8.1. The vertical line representing a minimal required (market) capital ratio does not limit asset risk or default risk on deposits. Both points *A* and *B* satisfy the capital constraint, yet the fair premium for deposit insurance at point *B* is 20 basis points, while at point *A* it is 10 basis points. Fully insured bank depositors will lend to banks at the riskless rate irrespective of bank risk. Thus, so long as deposit insurance premia do not fully reflect asset risk choices by banks, bank profits will be an increasing function of asset risk.

The Solution

The deficiencies of minimum capital requirements have led to continuing calls for further reforms to deposit insurance within the USA and elsewhere. Two of the most popular reforms that have been considered are 'narrow banking' and 'market discipline' (or required 'subordinated debt').

The narrow banking approach would restrict government insurance to a separately chartered narrow bank within the bank holding company, which would hold transparently low-risk, market-priced assets and issue insured deposits. The rest of the bank holding company's operations would be unregulated, and deposits held outside the narrow bank would be restricted to uninsured time deposits. Narrow banking effectively eliminates any risk to the government from insuring deposits and thus is simply another name for the suggestion that deposit insurance be repealed.

I have argued elsewhere (Calomiris, 1997) that, even if the repeal of deposit insurance were desirable on economic grounds (assuming, for example, that private coalitions of bankers could provide most or all of the social gains contemplated by a government-run safety net), narrow banking is not politically credible. Uninsured short-term deposits outside the narrow bank would still leave banks susceptible to capital losses and to the possibility of runs, which could be used to motivate ad hoc government interventions to protect uninsured deposits. Thus narrow banking does not repeal deposit insurance, it simply repeals all the prudential regulation and supervision that accompanies deposit insurance.

A subordinated debt-financing requirement can provide an alternative means of reforming deposit insurance. It has the advantage of ensuring incentive compatibility with a minimal set of regulatory guidelines and no reliance on government supervisors to analyse and disclose the condition of bank loan portfolios. Consider a rule that would require banks to finance a minimal fraction (say, 2 per cent) of their total non-reserve assets with subordinated debt (uninsured debt) earning a yield no greater than 50 basis points above the riskless rate.[3] That rule would force banks to operate below the 50 basis point risk schedule. If the most junior 2 per cent of debt bears a premium of 50 basis points, then overall the fairly priced risk premium for all debt (including the 98 per cent of debt that is insured) must be lower.

To be willing to hold the bank's debt, private subordinated debt holders would have to be satisfied that the leverage and the portfolio risk of the bank were sufficiently low to warrant that low (50 basis point) yield spread on debt. Banks that were unable to convince debt markets of the adequacy of their capital and the prudence of their investments would be unable to roll over some of their subordinated debt. Thus the subordinated debt ratio requirement naturally pushes banks to reduce their portfolio risk if it ever becomes excessive.[4]

The limitation on the yield spread serves the important purpose of limiting the risk on insured debt (which is senior to the subordinated debt) and allowing one to set deposit insurance premia at an actuarily fair rate – that is, one that reflects the true risk of default on insured deposits. Contingent claims pricing (based on the Black–Scholes model or some more realistic variant of that approach) can be used to derive the risk premium for insured debt from the observed yield on the subordinated debt.

In a world of increasing complexity and expanding opportunities for rapid increases in portfolio risk (via derivatives or emerging market securities) one of the most desirable features of a reliance on subordinated debt requirements is that they place the primary 'regulatory' and 'supervisory' burdens on sophisticated market participants with their own money at stake. Government regulators and supervisors have neither adequate skills nor sufficient incentives to monitor and control the condition of banks continuously.

Subordinated debt – or similar means of bringing private market discipline to bear on bank risk and capital choices – offers the only desirable solution to safety net incentive problems. The undesirable alternative is draconian restrictions on bank activities that try to limit risk taking by banks, in lending and elsewhere. In today's complex and competitive global banking environment, efficiency in banking is increasingly identified with broadening bank powers to enter new areas (Calomiris and Ramirez, 1996). Extreme restrictions on bank risk taking not only undermine the lending function of banks, they also translate into inefficient limitations on the menu of services banks can offer.

Others have noted the advantages of subordinated debt requirements over other ways to implement deposit insurance. The Federal Reserve Banks of Chicago and Atlanta developed, in the late 1980s, detailed proposals for implementing subordinated debt rules, which were greeted favourably within and outside the Federal Reserve System (Keehn, 1989; Wall, 1989). Nevertheless subordinated debt did not win the day politically in the USA or in the international debate over capital standards. In the case of the United States, the late 1980s were a time of high loan losses and scarce capital in banking, and banks lobbied successfully against increasing market discipline through an uninsured debt requirement.

Not only does the Basle (and the American) approach to capital standards avoid any subordinated debt requirement, it discriminates against subordinated debt. The Basle standards limit the extent to which tier 2 capital components (essentially, the sum of subordinated debt and preferred stock) can satisfy overall capital requirements, and also limit the extent to which subordinated debt can be used in the place of preferred stock to satisfy a tier 2 capital requirement.

Of course, there are pitfalls that must be avoided if subordinated debt is to promote private market discipline and eliminate the moral hazard problem posed by the government safety net. The two most important potential problems are the potential for a politically motivated 'bail out' of subordinated debt holders, and the potential for subordinated debt to be purposely overpriced by bank insiders who surreptitiously purchase the debt. While both of these problems are serious, they can be dealt with fairly well by easily implemented safeguards.

The potential for a bail-out of subordinated debt, of course, would undermine the whole effort to eliminate the moral hazard problem of deposit insurance, which rests on the imposition of losses (so-called 'haircuts') on uninsured debt holders. If subordinated debt is not really junior to the government insurer, it serves no purpose. It is widely believed that many governments provide implicit insurance for some or all uninsured debts in their banking systems. That raises the question of whether government is willing or able to allow private market discipline to take place. Calomiris (1997) argued that there are ways to limit the likelihood of a bail-out of subordinated debt by restricting the identities of the holders of subordinated debt to those that the government would be unlikely to bail out (for example, foreign-based banks) and by providing other systemic protections to the financial system that limit the incentive to provide bail-outs. Of course, there is no way to design a foolproof system of subordinated debt that can absolutely tie the hands of a government so as to permit private losses. That is not just a problem for subordinated debt proposals to reform deposit insurance; a government that will always bail out everyone will not be able to design any means for avoiding the subsidization of risk.

The second potential problem with a subordinated debt system is the potential for hidden, insider holdings of subordinated debt. Bank insiders would have an incentive to bid too high a price for subordinated debt, if they were permitted to do so. Since the banker is simply paying the excessive price to himself, he is indifferent to the loss from overpaying for the debt. But the banker gains from the lower cost of deposit insurance, which results from the government's reliance on private market pricing to constrain and measure bank risk taking. Thus, if insiders were permitted to hold subordinated debt, the yield paid for subordinated debt might bear little relationship to its true risk, and might be of little use in eliminating the problem of moral hazard.

A simple solution to this problem is to require that the holders of subordinated debt have no direct or indirect interest in the stock of the bank that issues the debt. The requirement that subordinated debt holders be unrelated foreign financial institutions might go a long way towards resolving the potential for insider holdings. Criminal and civil penalties for violating restrictions on the identities of subordinated debt holders would also be useful.

The idea of subordinated debt as a cure for abuse of the safety net has important historical precedents. As emphasized in much of the recent research on the operation of banks prior to the era of deposit insurance, holders of large amounts of bank debt (often other banks) helped to ensure the proper mix of assistance and discipline within the banking system (Gorton, 1985; Calomiris, 1989, 1990, 1993b; Calomiris and Gorton, 1991; Calomiris and Schweikart, 1991; Calomiris and Mason, 1997). They provided mutual assistance to solvent banks during times of illiquidity because they were knowledgeable about the banks' prospects and because debt holders faced strong incentives to help solvent banks. They also provided discipline for insolvent banks by helping to hasten their closure when that was warranted, again because large debt holders were able to observe the condition of banks, and because they faced a strong incentive to limit their losses as creditors.

LIMITED PROGRESS IN CHILE AND ARGENTINA

Chile after 1986

As noted above, Chile's banking collapse of 1982 predated by several years that of the USA. Chilean reforms, realized through a series of laws from November 1986 to August 1989 (Ramirez and Rosende, 1992; Brock, 1992, apps I and II; Budnevich, 1996), also predate the banking reform legislations of 1989 and 1991 in the USA. Those reforms followed an enormous government-financed bank recapitalization programme, which ended in 1986. The banking collapse and the costs of recapitalization produced a strong consensus to prevent a recurrence of the banking collapse by strengthening regulation and supervision to prevent abuse of the safety net.

As with the reforms that took place later in the USA, Chile reformed its capital requirements and sought ways to improve the credibility of government supervision and regulation. Like FDICIA, Chile's new laws emphasized the importance of early intervention by the government to shut down low-capital institutions. The Chileans did more than the USA, however, to ensure that capital requirements would be meaningful and enforced by regulators by bringing the private market into the supervisory process. They adopted aggressive market value accounting and required private supervision (auditing) of banks in addition to government supervision. Financial investments with more than a one-year maturity have to be repriced every month and marked to market. In addition to government supervision of internal risk ratings and valuations by the bank, two independent private auditors must examine each bank every year, and the results of their investigation are a matter of public record.

Reserve requirements are also high for Chilean banks. Demand deposits are subject to a 9 per cent reserve requirement, and all deposits in excess of 2.5 times bank capital accounts must be backed by a 100 per cent reserve deposit at the central bank. A special reserve requirement of 30 per cent is placed on foreign deposits (which are presumed to be more prone to withdrawal). The Chilean reforms also rolled back deposit insurance coverage, in a manner similar in effect to requiring some subordinated debt. Time deposits in banks receive only partial coverage, which means that, on the margin, private debt holders bear significant risk and therefore retain the incentive to monitor banks and punish imprudent behaviour.

Central Bank lending to commercial banks is limited to 60 per cent of the total amount of required reserves, and the cost of borrowing is a steeply increasing function of the amount borrowed. Most importantly, borrowing from the central bank cannot free a bank from having to comply with reserve and capital regulations.

The Superintendency is required to publish in a national newspaper three times a year a detailed report on each bank's compliance with capital requirements and the quality ratings of the bank's assets (which reflects explicit estimates of the probabilities of loss on those assets). The Superintendency is explicitly forbidden by law from delaying the recognition of losses in a bank's accounts. Regulators' opinions are a matter of public record. The only right of secrecy within the banking system is the right of depositor privacy.

If a bank is found to be in violation of its capital or liquidity requirements, its shareholders must immediately raise capital to comply with the law. Banks that cannot recapitalize must be closed, unless both their uninsured creditors and the Superintendency (which insures deposits) agree to restructure the bank. Because subordinated debt holders must approve any restructuring of banks, and because restructuring plans must be approved very quickly after the bank sinks below its minimum capital and reserve requirements, there is little opportunity or incentive for low-capital banks to adopt high-risk strategies after losing capital, since doing so would increase the incentive of subordinated debt holders to block a restructuring of the bank's liabilities to avoid liquidation.

If the uninsured debt holders of the bank are unwilling to rescue it, the law permits a consortium of other private banks to lend to the weak bank an uninsured loan which can be used to satisfy the weak bank's capital requirement.

The law is specifically designed to permit banks to limit negative externalities from systemic risks, and envisions banks establishing private regulatory clauses restricting the activities of the bank receiving assistance as part of the lending contract that preserves the institution.

Chilean law also emphasizes firewalls that legally separate the financing and risks of insured banks from those of non-depository affiliates. Furthermore banks are not permitted to hold stock in firms. While these regulations limit some potential economies of scope from mixing banking, investment banking and commerce (Calomiris and Ramirez, 1996), they have the important benefit of limiting the potential abuse of deposit insurance. As the experience of many countries has taught, permitting banks to own industrial conglomerates can concentrate political power to such an extent that it undermines the political will of government to enforce banking regulations. This in turn makes it possible for bank–industry conglomerates to abuse the financial safety net.

Despite many desirable and innovative features of the Chilean approach, in its essence it is still a capital-cum-intervention scheme for reforming the safety net and is thus very not different in intent from the Basle–FDICIA approach. Because the political credibility of 'partial' insurance is suspect, one could argue that there is no required subordinated debt financing. Neither is there any limit on the yield on uninsured bank deposits. The private audits mandated by law may be of some help, but one can question whether licensed auditors have the same strong incentives to discover and react to adverse information that subordinated debt holders have.

Still, the Chilean approach does better than FDICIA at putting protections in place that keep low- (or negative-) capital banks from abusing deposit insurance protection. The removal of privacy protections for bank borrowers, the stated commitment to the aggressive application of mark-to-market accounting, the requirement of independent audits, prohibitions on forbearance and the involvement of uninsured debt holders in the resolution of bank distress, all are intended to promote credible capital regulation. But, as shown in Figure 8.1, that does not translate into removing the potential for abuse of the safety net, because bank portfolio risks must also be controlled. That is especially worrying in an environment where derivatives and other important financial instruments offer the opportunities for banks to increase arbitrarily the riskiness of their portfolios (see also Edwards, 1996, pp. 164–7).

The Chilean bank regulations reflect an understanding of this problem. In addition to capital requirements, bank regulations limit or prohibit a variety of activities. Indeed, one could argue that the possibility of abuse of the safety net is not the largest social cost that comes from the Chilean approach. Of greater importance is the cost of restricting the scope, complexity and innovativeness of banks. Such costly limits are deemed necessary because of the potential for abuse of the safety net under the Chilean capital-cum-intervention approach to safety net reform, because allowing banks to pursue arbitrarily large, hard-to-measure portfolio risks encourages potential abuse of the safety net.

Argentina

Argentina experienced three waves of costly banking collapses in the 1980s, in 1980–82, 1985 and 1989. Combined with the continuing problems of poor macroeconomic growth and hyperinflation, these financial crises helped to propel reforms in the 1990s. Argentina adopted some of the reforms introduced in Chile, including strict disclosure requirements about bank credit quality, but, unlike Chile, opted for a more radical approach to banking reform. In 1992, deposit insurance was abolished (Miller, 1993). Some government-controlled financial institutions remained beyond the grasp of private market discipline, but private banks (which comprise the bulk of the financial system and include domestic banks of various sizes as well as large, global players like Citibank and Bank of Boston) were left to their own devices.

At the same time, as part of the same ambitious programme of financial liberalization and fiscal austerity, Argentina adopted a currency board – effectively relinquishing power to determine the domestic money supply. The role of the monetary authority became one of converting pesos and dollars into one another on demand. The banking system was permitted to offer deposits in either pesos or dollars (which trade at par with one another). Relinquishing monetary powers meant giving up the power to lend to banks via the discount window. Thus, by the early 1990s, Argentina had legislated away its ability to provide any government assistance to private banks via deposit insurance or central bank lending. When the Mexican 'tequila crisis' hit in 1994 and 1995, Argentina experienced massive outflows of deposits, initially confined to peso-denominated accounts (reflecting a lack of confidence in Argentina's currency board commitment). As the money supply imploded under the pressure of currency speculation, and the economy began to falter, depositors' attention shifted to the (endogenous) problem of credit quality in the banking system.

Some banks experienced large outflows of deposits, and the government allowed some of those banks to fail. But as the crisis wore on, the government began to soften its stand a little, reflecting growing political pressures. It provided open bank assistance to subsidize acquisitions of some troubled banks and it reintroduced deposit insurance, although limiting it to $10 000 per depositor. Studies of the banking crisis undertaken at the central bank indicated that the withdrawals of deposits from banks had not been random or irrational (Schumacher, 1997). The banks most likely to lose deposits and fail were those that were demonstrably weakest prior to the crisis. At the same time it also seemed that, in at least one or two cases, solvent banks had faced withdrawals that forced their closure. Thus, while the Argentines came away from the crisis with substantial confidence in the wisdom of private market discipline over banks, they also felt that there was a need to enhance the government's role in avoiding unnecessary liquidation.

Three important initiatives emerged from the experience of 1994–95. First, to improve the central bank's ability to provide liquidity to the financial system (without changing its commitment to a currency board), the central bank sought and arranged lines of credit from a consortium of international banks, to be used in times of crisis.

Second, the government turned its attention to the promotion of institutional reforms that would enhance credit risk transparency for banks and their loan customers, and thus possibly reduce potential problems of information asymmetry that promote unwarranted withdrawals from banks. Those reforms included bankruptcy reform, a new initiative to centralize collateral registration for bank loans and a centralized public database to publicize the fundamental characteristics of bank borrowers and the credit risks they pose for individual banks.

Finally, in November 1996, a new law was passed in Argentina requiring banks to finance 2 per cent of their total deposits in the form of subordinated debt. To my knowledge, Argentina is the only country to have instituted such a requirement. The subordinated debt requirement ensures that, even if a bank's other deposits are all insured, at least 2 per cent of its financing must satisfy the standards of the private market.

Unfortunately the law has not instituted all of the provisions envisioned above (see pp. 108–11). There is no maximum yield on subordinated debt and there is no attempt to link observed yields and the pricing of deposit insurance. One interpretation of the Argentine initiative is that it is an experiment to see how difficult it will be to create a new market for subordinated debt and to observe the yield structure of that market, before setting maximum yields and before relying too much on subordinated debt yields to determine insurance premia. Despite this modest beginning, Argentina's new approach may open a new chapter in the history of deposit insurance, one in which private market discipline acts in concert with government protection to allow incentive-compatible financial liberalization. The exciting prospect is that credible market discipline will permit banks to enter a richer array of activities without the fear that doing so will produce abuse of the safety net.

One of the most important factors that has allowed Argentina to embark on this ambitious programme of reforms is its historical openness to foreign banks. The presence of many important global banks in Argentina matters in several ways: it applies pressure on domestic banks to become competitive; it brings into the economy large, diversified banks which can provide stability during difficult macroeconomic times; and it helps to make sensible bank regulation and supervisory discipline easier, since bank–government relations are naturally more at arm's length. New Zealand's banking system is a more extreme case of an almost entirely foreign-owned banking system, which displays a similar commitment to regulatory discipline.

The recent banking crises in Mexico and Venezuela have led the Mexican and Venezuelan governments to loosen restrictions on foreign entry and there has been significant new entry by foreign banks into those countries. If the experiences of Argentina and New Zealand are any guide, this bodes well for the ability of Mexico and Venezuela to achieve more politically credible discipline over their banks.

CONCLUSION

This chapter has traced the history of the development of the modern bank safety net, the growing disillusion with bank safety nets internationally over the past decade, and potential reforms to safety net policies – notably subordinated debt requirements – which, it has been argued, may point the way to a stable and incentive-compatible 'post-modern' era of bank deregulation.

As the examples of Chilean and Argentine banking reforms illustrate, bringing credible private market discipline to bear on banks may allow developing countries to come to grips with the destabilizing influence of poorly managed safety nets by bringing credible private market discipline to bear on banks. The challenge remains one of implementing a mix of policies that will allow banks to provide innovative and efficient financial services while avoiding perverse incentives to government protection. Despite some shortcomings in the policies of both countries, Chile and Argentina have been among the most committed regulatory innovators in the search for bank stability and efficiency.

NOTES

1. New York City banks received very little protection from deposit insurance during the 1930s, since very few of their deposits were small enough to qualify for insurance.
2. Calomiris (1994) argues that, similarly, in the absence of asymmetric information problems, there would be no role for a central bank discount window to deal with financial problems occurring outside the banking system.
3. Off-balance-sheet activities could be included in the measure of total non-reserve assets, as is done currently in computing 'risk-weighted assets' under the Basle guidelines. Because the private market pricing of subordinated-debt issues of banks take all risks into account (including on-balance sheet-credit risk, off-balance-sheet credit risk, and market risks) the difficulty of ascertaining or limiting off-balance-sheet risks is a further motivation for reliance on subordinated debt.
4. The details of my subordinated debt proposal can be found in Calomiris (1997). There it is argued that overlapping generations of issues of certificates of deposit provide the most politically feasible means of credibly enforcing the subordinated debt requirement.

REFERENCES

Barth, James R. and Philip F. Bartholomew (1992), 'The Thrift Industry Crisis: Revealed Weaknesses in the Federal Deposit Insurance System', in James Barth and Dan Brumbaugh (eds), *The Reform of Federal Deposit Insurance*, New York: Harper Business, pp. 36–116.

Boyd, John and Mark Gertler (1994), 'The Role of Large Banks in the Recent U.S. Banking Crisis', *Federal Reserve Bank of Minneapolis Quarterly Review* (Winter),-2–21.

Brewer, Elijah, (1995), 'The Impact of the Current Deposit Insurance System on S&L Shareholders' Risk/Return Tradeoffs', *Journal of Financial Services Research*, **9**, 65–9.

Brewer, Elijah, and Thomas Mondschean (1993), 'Junk Bond Holdings, Premium Tax Offsets, and Risk Exposure at Life Insurance Companies', Working Paper 93-3, Federal Reserve Bank of Chicago.

Brewer, Elijah, Thomas Mondschean and Philip Strahan (1992), 'The Effect of Capital on Portfolio Risk at Life Insurance Companies', Working Paper 92-29, Federal Reserve Bank of Chicago.

Brock, Philip L. (ed.) (1992), *If Texas Were Chile: A Primer on Banking Reform*, San Francisco: ICS Press.

Budnevich, Carlos (1996), 'Banking System Regulation in Chile', Working Paper, Banco Central de Chile.

Calomiris, Charles W. (1989), 'Deposit Insurance: Lessons from the Record', *Federal Reserve Bank of Chicago Economic Perspectives* (May/June), 10–30.

Calomiris, Charles W. (1990), 'Is Deposit Insurance Necessary? An Historical Perspective', *Journal of Economic History*, **50**, 283–95.

Calomiris, Charles W. (1991), 'The Motives of U.S. Debt Management Policy, 1790–1880: Efficient Discrimination and Time Consistency', *Research in Economic History*, **13**, 67–105.

Calomiris, Charles W. (1992), 'Do "Vulnerable" Economies Need Deposit Insurance? Lessons from U.S. Agriculture in the 1920s', in P.L. Brock (ed.), *If Texas Were Chile: A Primer on Banking Reform*, San Francisco: ICS Press, pp. 237–314.

Calomiris, Charles W. (1993a), 'The Decline of Private Deposit Insurance in the United States: A Comment', *Carnegie–Rochester Conference Series on Public Policy*, **38**,-129–42.

Calomiris, Charles W. (1993b), 'Regulation, Industrial Structure, and Instability in U.S. Banking: An Historical Perspective', in Michael Klausner and Lawrence J. White (eds), *Structural Change in Banking*, Homewood, Ill.: Business One-Irwin, pp. 19–116.

Calomiris, Charles W. (1994), 'Is the Discount Window Necessary? A Penn Central Perspective', *Federal Reserve Bank of St Louis Review*, **76** (May/June), 31–55.

Calomiris, Charles W. (1997), 'Building an Incentive-Compatible Safety Net: Special Problems for Developing Countries', *Journal of Banking and Finance*, forthcoming.

Calomiris, Charles W. and Gary Gorton (1991), 'The Origins of Banking Panics: Models, Facts and Bank Regulation', in R. Glenn Hubbard (ed.), *Financial Markets and Financial Crises*, Chicago: University of Chicago Press, pp. 109–73.

Calomiris, Charles W. and Charles M. Kahn (1991), 'The Role of Demandable Debt in Structuring Optimal Banking Arrangements', *American Economic Review*, **81** (June), 497–513.

Calomiris, Charles W. and Joseph Mason (1997), 'Contagion and Bank Failures During the Great Depression: The June 1932 Chicago Banking Panic', *American Economic Review*, **87**, 863–83.

Calomiris, Charles W. and Carlos D. Ramirez (1996), 'The Role of Financial Relationships in the History of American Corporate Finance', *Journal of Applied Corporate Finance* **9** (Summer), 52–73.

Calomiris, Charles W. and Larry Schweikart (1991), 'The Panic of 1857: Origins, Transmission and Containment', *Journal of Economic History*, **51** (December), 807–34.

Calomiris, Charles W. and David C. Wheelock (1997), 'Was the Great Depression a Watershed in American Monetary History?', in M.C. Bordo, C. Goldin and E.N. White (eds), *The Defining Moment: The Great Depression and the American Economy in the Twentieth Century*, Chicago: University of Chicago Press pp. 23–66.

Calomiris, Charles W., and Eugene N. White (1994), 'The Origins of Federal Deposit Insurance', in C. Goldin and G.D. Libecap (eds), *The Regulated Economy: A Historical Approach to Political Economy*, Chicago: University of Chicago Press pp. 145–88.

Calomiris, Charles W. and Berry Wilson (1997), 'Bank Capital and Portfolio Management: The 1930s Capital Crunch and Scramble to Shed Risk', Working Paper, Columbia University.

Calomiris, Charles W., Charles M. Kahn and Stefan Krasa (1994), 'Optimal Contingent Bank Liquidation Under Moral Hazard', Working Paper, Columbia University.

Caprio, Gerard and Daniela Klingebiel (1996a), 'Bank Insolvency: Bad Luck, Bad Policy or Bad Banking', in Michael Bruno and Boris Pleskovic (eds), *Annual World Bank Conference on Development Economics, 1996*, Washington DC: The World Bank, pp. 79–114.

Caprio, Gerard and Daniela Klingebiel (1996b), 'Bank Insolvency: Cross-Country Experience', World Bank Policy Research Working Paper 1620, July.

Carey, Mark S. (1990), 'Feeding the Fad: The Federal Land Banks, Land Market Efficiency, and the Farm Credit Crisis', PhD dissertation, University of California, Berkeley.

de Krivoy, Ruth (1995), 'Lessons from Financial Crises: Evidence from Venezuela', *Proceedings of the 31st Annual Conference on Bank Structure and Competition*, Federal Reserve Bank of Chicago.

de la Cuadra, Sergio and Salvador Valdes (1992), 'Myths and Facts about Financial Liberalization in Chile: 1974–1983', in P.L. Brock (ed.), *If Texas Were Chile: A Primer on Banking Reform*, San Francisco: ICS Press, pp. 11–101.

Edwards, Franklin R. (1996), *The New Finance: Regulation and Financial Stability*, Washington, DC: AEI Press.

Flood, Mark (1992), 'The Great Deposit Insurance Debate', *Federal Reserve Bank of St Louis Review*, **76** (May/June), 51–77.

Garber, Peter (1997), 'Managing Risks to Financial Markets from Volatile Capital Flows: The Role of Prudential Regulation', Working Paper, Brown University.

Gorton, Gary (1985), 'Clearing Houses and the Origin of Central Banking in the United States', *Journal of Economic History*, **45** (June), 277–83.

Horvitz, Paul (1992), 'The Causes of Texas Bank and Thrift Failures', in P.L. Brock (ed.), *If Texas Were Chile: A Primer on Banking Reform*, San Francisco: ICS Press, pp.-131–60.

Kane, Edward (1989), *The S&L Insurance Mess: How Did It Happen?*, Washington DC: Urban Institute Press.

Kane, Edward (1992), 'The Incentive Incompatibility of Government-Sponsored Deposit Insurance Funds', in James Barth and Dan Brumbaugh (eds), *The Reform of Federal Deposit Insurance*, New York: Harper Business, pp. 144–66.

Keehn, Silas (1989), 'Banking on the Balance: Powers and the Safety Net, A Proposal,' Working Paper, Federal Reserve Bank of Chicago.

Lindgren, Carl-Johan, Gillian Garcia and Matthew I. Saal (1996), *Bank Soundness and Macroeconomic Policy*. Washington, DC: International Monetary Fund.

Mason, Joseph (1996), 'The Effects of Reconstruction Finance Corporation Assistance to Banks During the Great Depression', Working Paper, Office of the Comptroller of the Currency, Washington DC.

Miller, Geoffrey P. (1993), 'Politics of Deposit Insurance Reform: The Case of Argentina', *The University of Chicago Law School Roundtable*, 129–52.

Ramirez, Guillermo and Francisco Rosende (1992), 'Responding to Collapse: Chilean Banking Legislation after 1983', in P.L. Brock (ed.), *If Texas Were Chile: A Primer on Banking Reform*, San Francisco: ICS Press, pp. 193–216.

Schumacher, Liliana (1997), 'The Causes of Bank Failures in Argentina During the Tequila Crisis', Working Paper, Banco Central de la Republica Argentina.

Schwartz, Anna J. (1992), 'The Misuse of the Fed's Discount Window', *Federal Reserve Bank of St Louis Review*, **74**, (September/October), 58–69.

Wall, Larry D. (1989), 'A Plan for Reducing Future Deposit Insurance Losses: Puttable Subordinated Debt', *Federal Reserve Bank of Atlanta Economic Review* (July/August),-2–17.

Index